Lawyering from the Heart

ASPEN PUBLISHERS

LAWYERING
from the heart

DEBORAH KENN
Professor of Law
Syracuse University
College of Law

Wolters Kluwer
Law & Business

AUSTIN   BOSTON   CHICAGO   NEW YORK   THE NETHERLANDS

Aspen Publishers
Attn: Permissions Department
76 Ninth Avenue, 7th Floor
New York, NY 10011-5201

To contact Customer Care, e-mail customer.care@aspenpublishers.com, call 1-800-234-1660, fax 1-800-901-9075, or mail correspondence to:

Aspen Publishers
Attn: Order Department
PO Box 990
Frederick, MD 21705

Printed in the United States of America.

1 2 3 4 5 6 7 8 9 0

ISBN 978-07355-8652-9

Kenn, Deborah, 1955-
   Lawyering from the heart / Deborah Kenn.
      p. cm.
   ISBN 978-0-7355-8652-9
   1. Public interest law — United States. 2. Practice of law — United States.
3. Kenn, Deborah, 1955- 4. Law teachers — United States — Biography. I. Title.
   KF299.P8K46 2009
   344.73 — dc22   2009023690

About Wolters Kluwer Law & Business

Wolters Kluwer Law & Business is a leading provider of research information and workflow solutions in key specialty areas. The strengths of the individual brands of Aspen Publishers, CCH, Kluwer Law International and Loislaw are aligned within Wolters Kluwer Law & Business to provide comprehensive, in-depth solutions and expert-authored content for the legal, professional and education markets.

CCH was founded in 1913 and has served more than four generations of business professionals and their clients. The CCH products in the Wolters Kluwer Law & Business group are highly regarded electronic and print resources for legal, securities, antitrust and trade regulation, government contracting, banking, pension, payroll, employment and labor, and healthcare reimbursement and compliance professionals.

Aspen Publishers is a leading information provider for attorneys, business professionals and law students. Written by preeminent authorities, Aspen products offer analytical and practical information in a range of specialty practice areas from securities law and intellectual property to mergers and acquisitions and pension/benefits. Aspen's trusted legal education resources provide professors and students with high-quality, up-to-date and effective resources for successful instruction and study in all areas of the law.

Kluwer Law International supplies the global business community with comprehensive English-language international legal information. Legal practitioners, corporate counsel and business executives around the world rely on the Kluwer Law International journals, loose-leafs, books and electronic products for authoritative information in many areas of international legal practice.

Loislaw is a premier provider of digitized legal content to small law firm practitioners of various specializations. Loislaw provides attorneys with the ability to quickly and efficiently find the necessary legal information they need, when and where they need it, by facilitating access to primary law as well as state-specific law, records, forms and treatises.

Wolters Kluwer Law & Business, a unit of Wolters Kluwer, is head-quartered in New York and Riverwoods, Illinois. Wolters Kluwer is a leading multinational publisher and information services company.

This book is dedicated to my parents, Lester J. and Marion Kenn. Their hearts no longer beat in the physical realm, but their unconditional love and inspiration live on.

TABLE OF CONTENTS

ACKNOWLEDGMENTS

This book would not have been possible without strong support from the Syracuse University College of Law, especially Dean Hannah Arterian. Part of that support was in the form of excellent research assistance from Brad Defoe and Jillian Farrar.

Editing expertise from Paul Frazier was invaluable, as were comments and suggestions from Benita Kenn, Robin Paul Malloy, Rob Nassau, and Jim Sicherman.

I am exceedingly grateful to the soulful lawyers, willing to take time from their busy lawyering lives, to be interviewed for this book. The stories of their lives, the work they do, and what motivates them, will impact me, my teaching, and my lawyering, forever.

The cover scales of justice concept was inspired by my dear friend, artist, and heartful lawyer, Chris Hickey.

Many thanks go to Rick Mixter and Dana Wilson of Aspen Publishers for their expert assistance, good humor, and strong support in an otherwise intimidating process.

Last, but not least, I thank John Dunkle, the lion-hearted, for the hours of listening, the deep guidance, and the companionship on this journey into the heart's wisdom.

Lawyering from the Heart

CHAPTER 1

The Foundation

In the fall of 1989, after more than eight years of practicing public interest law, I accepted a teaching position at the Syracuse University College of Law in its clinical legal education program. Details of my journey to this place and time will unfold later but, for purposes of introduction, I will say that I have been incredibly privileged to teach and direct the Community Development Law Clinic for these 20 years. Supervising student attorneys on cases involving economic development in low-income neighborhoods renews my passion for economic and social justice every day. To say that I am grateful to spend my time in an endeavor I truly love, and in which I continue to grow and learn, is an understatement. To be living my values, to be using my legal skills bringing some modicum of justice to a legal system that is reflective of society's most destructive power imbalances and greatest injustices, and to be encouraging law students to consider doing the same, is far beyond anything I would have allowed myself to dream, even in my wildest dreams, when I graduated law school in 1980, intent on public interest lawyering. These past 29 years give testament to my love of the mystery of life and an affirmation of my belief in the unknown forces that guide us.

To be exposing law students to communities of people who, for the most part, they never have — and never would have — encountered in life and witnessing the beneficial transformation of their prejudice, stereotypes, and perspectives, are rewards in and of themselves. But it is even more gratifying to then explore and examine with the student attorneys I teach ways to use the law to create and foster opportunities for people and communities who lack access to even the most basic means of survival.

There exist, of course, harsh realities, even in the wildest of one's dreams. Teaching primarily third-year law students, I witness firsthand their struggles and challenges during their job searches. Watching and guiding these eager souls in their search for meaningful employment can be excruciatingly painful. The challenges and obstacles seem insurmountable at times, especially for students wanting to pursue public interest law. As we move through challenging economic times where law firm lay-offs, recissions of offers to recent graduates, and deferrals of start dates for first year associates are becoming far too common,[1] it is hard for any graduate to remain optimistic, and the competition for public interest law employment intensifies. It is difficult watching all of my students endure the hopes and rejections, opportunities and challenges of searching for their first job. From my vantage point, I know it will turn out okay for them. That assurance, though, is little consolation while they're searching. The students seeking public interest law jobs have an additional hurdle to overcome. During my 20 years of teaching law, I've heard far too many times the voices of third-year

---

1. "3Ls Do the Grim Math on the Job Market: Grads to Vie with Newly Laid Off," *National Law Journal* (April 17, 2009), www.law.com/jsp/nlj/PubArticleNLJ.jsp?id=1202429976215.

law students saying, "You know, when I first got to law school I really wanted to pursue public interest law but now that I'm a third-year law student and I'm thousands of dollars in debt, and public interest jobs pay so little, I just can't." This lament conforms to national data indicating that over two-thirds of law students who originally intended to pursue public interest law jobs do not do so, with some studies concluding that up to 76 percent of law students intending to go into public interest or government jobs do not end up doing so.[2] The assurance, "it will turn out okay," falls on closed ears for students balancing their desire to be public interest lawyers with their seemingly insurmountable debt. They look at me incredulously, and I can only imagine what they would say to me if there were no consequences!

My own frustration and struggle has been with the "I can't." Tell me you've decided not to; tell me it's too hard; tell me you're not willing to face the sacrifices; tell me the dog ate your karmic homework; but it pains my heart to hear "I can't," that you're denying yourself the pursuit of a dream and work you can be passionate about for financial reasons. A few years ago, after hearing one too many "I can'ts," I decided to write about those who can and do; those who have persevered; who have said, "Yes, I can." The pages of this book include stories of 22 public interest lawyers, in varying stages of their careers, who have followed their passions, using their legal skills to help others. My goal was to be able to have more than the empty assurance, "Don't worry, it will be okay" for my students who wish to pursue public interest law; to be able to tell the stories of those brave souls who have said, "Yes, I can and I have and I will continue to do so."

In addition, to my surprise and relief, since conducting these interviews, Congress has finally taken on the issue of the cost of

---

2. Christa McGill, "Educational Debt and Law Student Failure to Enter Public Service Careers: Bringing Empirical Data to Bear," 31 *Law and Social Inquiry* 677 (2006): 698-701. *See also* Amy Bradshaw, "Exploring Law Students' Attitudes, Beliefs, and Experiences About the Relationship Between Business Law and Public Interest Law," 20 *Wisconsin Women's Law Journal* 287 (Fall 2005): 292, saying: "Today, less than three percent of graduating law students go into public interest employment — far fewer students than the number who cite the opportunity to serve the public interest as a reason for attending law school."

college and graduate schools and the problems faced by those professionals wanting to work in public interest careers. In September 2007, a generous loan forgiveness program for people in many types of public interest jobs, including public interest law jobs, was passed by both Houses of Congress by a veto-proof majority and then signed by President Bush.[3] For law students dreaming of entering public interest law after graduation, that dream has become more affordable.

The lawyers whose stories are told in the following pages are all the more heroic for having stayed true to their ideal of giving back to a world that did not support them in their quest for justice; the world before our nation took this major step to recognize commitment to the public good. Those who come after them, with the benefit of loan forgiveness, should have an easier journey. Lessening the education debt factor, they need only look in the mirror of their hearts, see within, face their values, and decide their path. Whatever they see and decide can be supported. The important factor now is that educational debt cannot be used as an excuse for not pursuing a dream or be viewed as an obstacle that can't be overcome. There will be more clarity in finding one's path, uncluttered by the insurmountable debt debris.

It still won't be easy. Even with loan forgiveness possibilities, public interest lawyering does not pay well. Although public interest lawyers can eventually end up with well-paying jobs and comfortable lifestyles, the path of seeking justice does not come with a guarantee of financial security. Especially for lawyers at the beginning of a public interest career, a choice must be made. The lawyers whose stories lie within the following pages are the role models who faced that decision when the choice was harder. They exemplify the type of people who are cited in many studies that indicate the rewards from following your heart's passion are far

---

3. The College Cost Reduction Act of 2007, Public Law 84, 110th Cong., 2d Sess. (September 29, 2007).

greater than any monetary rewards gained from denying the pursuit of your dream.[4]

This book endeavors to support everyone who follows their passion in life, whatever the monetary compensation. Because the path of following one's heart and listening to that voice within becomes more challenging the lower the pay scale, the stories here focus on people who had to choose passion over a bigger paycheck. For the lawyers who face choices and for those who can have it all, passion and a sizeable paycheck, there are challenges. One's heart sometimes whispers inaudibly and the task becomes finding ways to turn up the volume to make difficult decisions on what path to take in this life. Hopefully, the stories in this book will be inspirational and an encouragement to those able to comfortably pursue passionate work without financial sacrifice. For those others of you in the position of many people, including law students, deciding between following your heart and following a paycheck, this book is meant to help you process that decision and provide role models to whom you might be able to relate.

For the purposes of this book, I interviewed mostly lawyers working in civil legal services and legal aid offices. I did this for two reasons. First, I think of civil legal services and legal aid as the lowest common denominator of public interest law work. The pay is less than government jobs and most other not-for-profit law firms,[5] it's not a "stepping stone" as are most public defender jobs, and the level of commitment required is unrelenting and demanding. Although the pay scales usually reward longevity in legal services and legal aid offices, even the longtime attorneys are earning less than a first-year associate, right out of law school, at some of the bigger law firms, who have in the recent past earned $165,000 a year to start and now with the reported consequences of the recession, are earning $130,000 to $145,000 to start.[6] The second reason for my

---

4. Stephanie Francis Ward, *infra* Note 19, and Jonathan Haidt, *infra* Notes 26 and 37.

5. *2006 Public Sector & Public Interest Salary Report* (National Assoc. of Law Professionals 2006).

6. Gina Passarella, "How Low Could Associate Salaries Go?," *National Law Journal* (April 8, 2009), www.law.com/jsp/nlj/PubArticleNLJ.jsp?id=1202429748242.

choice of interviewees is that my background is in legal services. My professional experience has offered many opportunities to meet and get to know attorneys working for legal services and legal aid offices. I made my way interviewing attorneys I knew and attorneys I got to know throughout the metropolitan New York City area (Manhattan, the South Bronx, East Brooklyn, and East Harlem); Chicago, Illinois; Albany and Syracuse, New York; the state support center for legal services in Rochester, New York; a civil rights law office in Chicago, and a not-for-profit affordable housing development organization in Chicago to interview the attorneys in this book.

The experience of writing this book has proven powerful and rewarding. It's definitely been an example of following my heart, and listening to my soul, despite the risks. And, as is usually the case, the calling I had to write this book has given me great rewards. Never have I been so intellectually inspired, emotionally moved, and spiritually energized in my research and writing. Each of the lawyers I interviewed spoke of his or her passion for helping others: the rewards of lawyering for the benefit of people who would not otherwise have access to our system of justice. Each, in his or her own way, repeated the sentiment, "I can't imagine doing anything else." In each case, dedication prevailed, despite the low pay and considerable education debt. Moreover, all of the lawyers interviewed had a variety of legal employment options they could have pursued after law school, including choices that offered higher pay and the potential for a more luxurious lifestyle. All of them were good law students — some went to Ivy League schools. But, ultimately, all deliberately chose lower paying job opportunities so they could pursue the work that fed their passion, not their wallets.

My goal in sharing the lives of these dedicated lawyers is not just sharing insights on how to live on public interest salaries. My main goal is to inspire those already highly motivated and those even remotely motivated to work for the betterment of society: Listen to that voice inside, however muffled or whispered it might be. That voice might just be the voice of your heart, beckoning you to fan the fires of your passion and follow a path showered with the deepest rewards this brief life has to offer.

CHAPTER 2

The Journey

A. THE VISION

Passion sings the song of the soul. Passion softens the heart. Passion lights up our minds with sparks of creativity. Passion connects us with our innermost reason for being alive. And, sometimes, yes, sometimes, passion pays the bills.

Imagine a world where following our heart's passion, connecting with our true, authentic self, and honoring each other's unique paths, were encouraged and supported. Imagine a world where fulfilling our deepest purpose and expressing our authenticity were valued more highly than making money and feeding our egos; a world in which filling our hearts didn't mean emptying our stomachs. Imagine a world where a passion for helping and supporting others, not only in surviving, but in "care gifting" to the world, could not only bring gratitude and emotional satisfaction to our lives but also financially support us. Imagine us all cooperating and collaborating to solve endemic societal issues that have gripped our nation.

Such a world does not have to be imagined. It is not evident in the mainstream of our society but it thrives, against all odds and with much persistence, in the lives of a few courageous, amazing souls determined to follow their hearts' desires and deep yearnings to help others.

Contrary to popular belief, this world exists among lawyers, in a loosely organized community of people we call public interest lawyers. In a society where the most spontaneous image of a lawyer is that of an ocean-dwelling predator with big jaws and teeth, with an unlimited thirst for blood; where jokes about lawyers suggest that their ethics are comparable to those of the devil,[7] there exists a small cadre of participants in the profession who have followed their hearts and their dreams in making the world a better place. It is a phenomenon some refer to as a "calling," to help those in our society who would otherwise not have access to our system of justice. The people, whether we refer to them as the disadvantaged, the have-nots, the poor, or the underprivileged, are folks just like anyone else. Through luck of the draw, accident, or choice of birth, they have not had the same opportunities: options for quality education, adequate health care, affordable, livable housing, and viable employment that folks in the middle and upper classes have had. Were it not for public interest lawyers working to help them access the limited opportunities for subsistence that are often denied to them, people who

---

7. The devil visited a lawyer's office and made him an offer. "I can arrange some things for you," the devil said. "I'll increase your income five-fold. Your partners will love you; your clients will respect you; you'll have four months of vacation each year and live to be a hundred. All I require in return is that your wife's soul, your children's souls, and their children's souls rot in hell for eternity." The lawyer thought for a moment. "What's the catch?" he asked. Rick M, posting to Lawyer-Jokes, posted on February 6, 2003, to http://www.lawyer-jokes.us (accessed on December 8, 2008).

couldn't begin to afford an attorney would not hope for what most of us take for granted in life. Were it not for public interest lawyers working to improve the lives of low-income people through systemic change on a broader scale, the status quo of opportunity, only for those born or bred into it, would remain unchallenged.

There exist untold numbers of ways to follow your calling. The spectrum of lawyering options between selfless public interest lawyering for the benefit of others and bloodthirsty, ruthless lawyering without a heart is vastly wide. The image of lawyers in exaggerated jokes is unfair to the majority of lawyers who live their day-to-day legal careers with ethical, professional, and civil codes of conduct similar to most people seeking to earn an honest day's wages and sleep soundly with clear consciences. This book contains stories, anecdotes, and factual information singing the praises of public interest lawyers, but it is meant to celebrate all those lawyers and others who listen to their hearts, find their calling, and follow their passion despite the not-so-subtle messages of society to conform to what's expected of you by others and ignore any voice that is not the logical output of analytical thinking.

Two very passionate lawyers I know, who are not public interest lawyers, come to mind immediately. A colleague who has dedicated his life to the practice and teaching of tax law remains a staunch defender of the heartfelt joy that comes from an area of practice normally reserved for the most reserved among the profession. My colleague instills his students with this passion, a passion for the Internal Revenue Code they take with them along with the saying he coined, "One Nation Under Code." My professor friend has even gotten t-shirts printed with his beloved slogan and many alumni make donations to the law school primarily to receive a t-shirt in return and honor their favorite professor, who happens to love tax law. He was a tax lawyer for the Wall Street elite before deciding his passion for tax law was contagious and he needed to infect as many law students with it as possible.

Similarly, a former student of mine now owns his own real estate law firm in lower Manhattan, employs more than 25 people, and practices real estate law for commercial and high-end developers with a passion and energy unparalleled in the business. This former student with his law firm earns millions of dollars, provides exemplary legal assistance to his clients, and he does so from the heart, without apology, on the path of his calling in life.

This book commends all who step out on a limb, royally compensated or not, but examines the characteristics and elements of the lives of those choosing to step out on a limb without a financial safety net. We sometimes call them social change lawyers. They use their legal education and skills to change the dynamics of a society that, for the most part, does not like to see the poorest among us; a society that has deliberately residentially segregated the poor so that the problem of poverty can be ignored;[8] a society that has historically created and maintained a callousness toward poverty that is unparalleled in the developed world. The social change lawyers' task might seem quixotic, but that does not deter them. They are tireless and selfless in their quest for social and economic justice for their clients and for low-income communities. The day-by-day small successes sustain them during the long-haul struggles for change that they are committed to achieving and they are sustained by their dreams of a more just society.

Just think, if lawyers can do good, anyone can! Many lawyers, not just public interest lawyers, do much that benefits the world. Lawyers who do not aspire to public interest careers can commit innumerable hours to pro bono cases, sit on boards of not-for-profit corporations, and dedicate themselves to any number of volunteer community services. The following pages include stories of lawyers who have committed their lives to public interest law, but there are many stories that could have been told of lawyers working in the mainstream who supplement their work with work in the public interest, do untold acts of community service, and live compassionately and kindly every day of their lives. The stories held within these pages are meant to inspire public interest in all professions

---

8. Douglas Massey and Nancy Denton, *American Apartheid: Segregation and the Making of the Underclass* (Harvard University Press 1993).

and employment, to whatever extent possible and comfortable for each individual.

We find the deepest fulfillment and live with the strongest passion when we open up to and grow into the unique gifts we are given in this life. As stated by the Honorable James Graves, Jr., addressing a law school graduating class, "In the measure of a man, the tape goes around the heart, not the head."[9] Finding work we can be passionate about (some might call it our soul work) leads to the greatest fulfillment and joy in life and can bring about real change in the lives of everyone with whom we come in contact. Even if you do not believe in a higher purpose for life, if you're seeking meaningful employment and a satisfying career, taking direction from the messages of an open heart, listening to your gut, some might say, leads to work about which you can be passionate. If each of us were to open the doorway through our hearts, hear the true calling of our souls, and follow that inner guidance, the world could be the better place everyone is seeking.

B. THE PATH

We live at a crossroads in human time. Our industrialized and technologized world has witnessed the power of destruction and creation. Some say that a historical imbalance toward destruction has brought us to the crossroads. The damaging costs of our quest for domination, consumption, and external power are obvious to many. Visionary thinkers profess that, without a deliberate and conscious shift toward the forces of creation and healing, our planet and its inhabitants might not survive. The need for this transformation of human society and endeavor to save the planet and her inhabitants has slowly made its way into our collective consciousness through such luminaries as 2007 Nobel Peace Prize winner Al Gore, in his multimedia undertaking *An Inconvenient Truth*, and

---

9. Justice James Graves, Jr., Mississippi Supreme Court Judge, Commencement Address at Syracuse University College of Law (May 20, 2007).

David C. Korten, in his groundbreaking book *The Great Turning.* Korten beseeches us to:

> Break the trance, replace the values of an inauthentic culture with the values of an authentic culture grounded in a love of life rather than a love of money, and people will realign their life energy and bring forth the life-serving institutions of a new era. The key is to change the stories by which we define ourselves. It is easier said than done, but I have found it to be a powerful strategic insight.[10]

Korten lays out the need for human society to commit to a cultural, economic, and political turning. He explains that the economic and political shift must follow a cultural change "from money and material excess to life and spiritual fulfillment, from relationships of domination to relationships of partnership, from a belief in our limitations to a belief in our possibilities, and from fearing our differences to rejoicing in our diversity."[11] It is Korten's belief that once the cultural turning has occurred, we will then transition to economic policies for the benefit of all, rather than some, and democratic principles based on cooperation rather than competition. Korten urges:

> Now as never before we must unleash the creative potential of the species and direct it to democratizing our cultures and institutions and bringing ourselves into balance with one another and Earth. It is the greatest creative challenge the species has ever faced. Success would seem a futile dream, except that all around the planet momentum is already building.[12]

---

10. David C. Korten, *The Great Turning: From Empire to Earth Community* (Berrett-Koehler Publishers 2006), 18.

11. *Id.* at 22.

12. *Id.*

The lawyers working to transform the world, of whom this book provides representatives, have found a way to make a positive contribution to our current society and impact the future of the world. Through the selfless work they accomplish and through their personal journeys of courage and authenticity, they are changing the world. Some prefer to remain anonymous, most are identified by their real names, but all of their stories are ones that inspire us to redefine ourselves individually and as a society and bring us together to build better communities.

In their own ways, each of the lawyers I interviewed spoke of their work as emanating from their hearts and souls as their purpose in this life. Believing that our heartfelt purpose is our highest purpose for being in this life, this *raison d'être* beckons to us at different times and in different ways. Whether we believe in the guidance of a supreme being, or a force that works beyond our comprehension, or have no belief in the great beyond but an awareness of the unknowable; whether we are religious, spiritual, agnostic, or pagan; whether we revel in the mystery of life or cower in fear at the great unknown; we all seek meaning in our lives. One needs look only to the mainstream online job search engine, Monster.com, as a reflection of what people looking for employment seek. Monster.com's motto, expressed on their home page, is "Your calling is calling."[13] It is through the doorway of the heart that we enter the house of soul.

C. THE GUIDANCE

The journey to our calling begins with hearing the soft voice of our heart's longing and the soul's beckoning, guiding us through that mystery, through the unknown, toward the deepest meaning of our lives. As understood by Deepak Chopra, visionary and writer, "The soul is really a junction point between time and the

---

13. www.monster.com

timeless."[14] Chopra believes that suffering occurs when a person ignores the guidance of his or her soul and becomes disconnected from the source, the true meaning of life. He says:

> Someone who is attuned to the soul begins to perceive that a subtle guidance is at work. The soul is silent; therefore it cannot compete with the contentious voices heard in the mind. You can spend years overshadowed by anger, fear, greed, ambition, and all the other distractions of inner life, but none of that activity touches Atman [soul]. The soul has its own project in mind.[15]

As illustrated by the lives of the lawyers in this book, those who listen to their heart and follow the beckoning of the soul can find a fulfillment and satisfaction that can only be described as extraordinary. It is not without challenges and obstacles. The limited income and extreme educational debt, in some cases paying off tens of thousands of dollars of educational loans, is no small part of that challenge. But the exultation at being the truest to ourselves and the greatest we can be supports us through the challenges and helps us over the obstacles. If we fail to follow our true calling because of the challenges, we sometimes pay a higher price. In the words of Steven Foster and Meredith Little, "Those without a meaningful life story all too easily trap themselves in nets fashioned by others to ensnare them, or they are swallowed up in their own thrashing."[16] Although there are many ways to follow one's calling as a lawyer and find meaning and authenticity in work, there are many well-documented accounts of the general malaise and misery that lawyers feel about the lack of meaning and satisfaction in their

---

14. Deepak Chopra, *How to Know God: The Soul's Journey Into the Mystery of Mysteries* (Three Rivers Press, 2001), 275.

15. *Id.* at 280.

16. Steven Foster and Meredith Little, *The Book of the Vision Quest: Personal Transformation in the Wilderness* (Simon & Schuster 1992), 21.

work.[17] This ennui reflects many people in society and, in Chopra's words:

> We all know the powerful addiction of money, power, career, and ego needs of every type. This momentum has kept suffering alive despite the enormous changes in human existence from age to age. Against this momentum the soul provides a means of solving every cause of pain.[18]

It's interesting to note that a survey of lawyers conducted by the American Bar Association in 2007 found that almost 70 percent of all public-sector lawyers conveyed satisfaction with their jobs, as opposed to only 44 percent of lawyers working in big firms.[19] Following one's heart, the core-driven passion one can feel for a particular calling, might alleviate the pain and boredom, and instill life with meaning and purpose.

Or, as spoken by Tom Robbins's character, Stubblefield, in his novel, *Villa Incognito*:

> In the end, perhaps we should simply imagine a joke, a long joke that's being continually retold in an accent too thick and too strange to ever be completely understood. Life is that joke, my friends. The soul is the punch line.[20]

---

17. Jean Stefancic and Richard Delgado, *How Lawyers Lose Their Way: A Profession Fails Its Creative Minds* (Duke University Press 2005), 53-59; Patrick J. Schiltz, "On Being a Happy, Healthy, and Ethical Member of an Unhappy, Unhealthy, and Unethical Profession," 52 *Vanderbilt Law Review* 871 (May 1999): 876.

18. Chopra, *supra* note 14, 282.

19. Stephanie Francis Ward, "Pulse of the Legal Profession," *ABA Journal* (October 2007): 34. These findings are similar to a Michigan Law School survey in the early 1990s finding that 42 percent of graduates working in private practice were quite satisfied with their work five years after graduation, as compared to 72 percent of their counterparts working as public interest lawyers. Schiltz, *supra* note 17.

20. Tom Robbins, *Villa Incognito* (No Exit Press 2004): 79.

People take many paths to the punch line. There exist many ways to express it once it's found. This book recognizes, illuminates, and celebrates the soulful lawyers who keep smiling through the joys, rewards, challenges, and obstacles of public interest work. In service to the world, their contribution is invaluable. For the majority of law students and lawyers who choose a path different than public interest work, I proclaim no judgment. I do not, in any way, want to contribute to the polarity and divisiveness of the world by judging people's paths as "good" or "bad." To do so would be counterproductive to the message of this book. I simply wish to celebrate the path of public interest law. Lawyers can find many ways to be of service to the world. One of the greatest thrills of being a clinical law professor is when a former student who has gone into corporate law at one of the behemoth for-profit law firms contacts me for advice on a case they've taken pro bono, representing a not-for-profit community organization. Many for-profit corporations approach our societal problems with creativity and a determination to be a positive force in healing our world and our planet and can treat their employees with great respect and dignity in the process. We are celebrating public interest law in its ability to be an inclusive, healing, positive power from within, not needing to consume, overpower, or exclude other creative, healing forces.

Now that Congress has passed the College Cost Reduction Act, perhaps the goals of social and economic justice are more attainable. The federal loan forgiveness program is a major first step in perpetuating national values that sustain opportunity for everyone. Finally, a break for those tireless souls who work in the public interest and the too often forgotten people of our collective public in whose interest they work. Perhaps this groundbreaking legislation reflects the beginning of an attitudinal change necessary to achieve economic and social justice for all. As expressed by Marianne Williamson in her book, *The Healing of America:*

> There is so much injustice in America, and such a
> conspiracy not to discuss it; so much suffering, and

so much deflection lest we notice. We are told that these problems are secondary, or that it would cost too much to fix them — as though money is what matters most. Greed is considered legitimate now, while brotherly love is not. Millions of us see this as an unacceptable violation of spiritual truth. We must create the restoration of our collective conscience, and turn it into political will.[21]

Perhaps the lawyering from the heart that is practiced by the people within these pages will combine forces with other work in the public interest to help reshape the soul of our nation. There is reason to hope.

D. THE BOOK

The first portion of this book, the journey into soulful lawyering from the heart, will explore the "calling" followed and path taken by several public interest lawyers. Guided by their hearts and passion to pursue public interest work, they are undeterred by the fears and restrictions of ego concerns. Next, I examine the obstacles along the path, including the cost of legal education, the lack of support for public interest work at most law schools and in the legal profession, societal factors that devalue public interest work, and the more general economic constraints of middle-class people trying to make financial ends meet. This portion of the book explores factors, programs, and perspectives that exist to help ease the climb over the obstacles and assist those brave enough to keep climbing. Once the obstacles are detailed, the rewards of following the calling and staying on the path guided by the heart are illuminated. Finally, recommendations for supporting public interest work are given. At the core of this exploration are the stories; the personal accounts

---

21. Marianne Williamson, *The Healing of America* (Simon & Schuster 1997), 24-25.

of people's lives that will move us, excite us, and serve as the contextual inspiration that, in the telling, can help us redefine ourselves as a society.

Lawyering from the Heart gives voice to the stories, reveals the hearts, and captures the souls of public interest lawyers. It reveals their commitment and endurance, especially in the face of the enormous cost of a legal education and the low wages of public interest jobs. It illustrates the incredible rewards of the work. It offers a challenge to the legal profession, legal educators, and society to better support the work of bringing justice to our neighbors who are sorely in need of social and economic opportunities. *Lawyering from the Heart* seeks to inspire potential and current law students and lawyers to look deep into their cores, follow their hearts, and accept the challenges and rewards of utilizing their legal educations for the benefit of others, to make the world a better place for us all.

3

The Calling

A. HEARING THE VOICE WITHIN

Lucky are the few who feel the calling from an early age, those who, guided in their lives by unseen, unknowable forces, trust the feelings and voices within and follow their calling to create satisfying lives and careers. At the other end of the soul-searching spectrum are those who, due to a variety of factors and life circumstances, cannot find purpose in a seemingly meaningless world. The majority of us reside in the middle of the spectrum where the guideposts in life are blurry. We must squint to see the fine print and stretch our abilities to translate the language of the heart and follow our deepest calling. Perhaps we find guidance to our heart's desire in a dream. Perhaps the serendipity of life provides us with an unavoidable opportunity. Some of us find mentors or role models who help guide us to the work of our hearts; often our parents, relatives, or friends unwittingly accept the position of guide. Those who try and work hard to hear and speak the language of the heart can spark its passion. By meditating or spending time alone in nature, seeking to open our hearts and listen inside to our instincts, the mind can be quieted and the voice of the heart made stronger. Life's journey can be a never-ending quest for a truly integrated self, a daily challenge to make the most of the mind, body, heart, and soul bestowed on us.

Our souls are mysterious beings. They seldom speak to us; when they do, their language is unintelligible. To truly attain authenticity we need to listen to our hearts, decipher the language of the soul within us, and hear its calling. But the societal toolbox of self-awareness contains mostly ego hammers and personality pliers. Our hearts and souls live in a world of Phillips-head screws and we are holding regular flathead screwdrivers. Unlocking the mysteries of our hearts and souls requires creativity, insight, patience, and, above all, desire.

Even when we are in touch with the longings of our hearts, when we can hear the calling to what will fulfill us and satisfy our passion, when the signposts along the way become surprisingly clear, our egos can bombard us with doubts and fears. If we find the work we are passionate about but that work doesn't pay well, our egos worry endlessly about paying the bills, about approaching financial ruin, homelessness, and hunger. Listening closely and our ability to dig deep and trust our inner wisdom is what's needed to sing the passion strongly and calm the ego concerns. Even now, as I write these words, my ego is chattering away about the risks. That not-so-little voice in my head says, "What are you, crazy? You really think people want to hear about lawyering from the heart? What a crazy idea anyway! Geez, Deb, you've got a great job with tenure, a comfortable lifestyle, why are you writing this book? Does the name 'Socrates' and the word 'hemlock' mean anything to you?"

As instructed by Eckhart Tolle in his groundbreaking work *A New Earth: Awakening to Your Life's Purpose*:

> To end the misery that has afflicted the human condition for thousands of years, you have to start

with yourself and take responsibility for your inner state at any given moment. That means now. . . . The moment you become aware of a negative state within yourself, it does not mean you have failed. It means that you have succeeded. Until that awareness happens, there is identification with inner states, and such identification is ego. With awareness comes dis-identification from thoughts, emotions, and reactions. This is not to be confused with denial. The thoughts, emotions, or reactions are recognized, and in the moment of recognizing, disidentification happens automatically. Your sense of self, of who you are, then undergoes a shift: Before you were the thoughts, emotions, and reactions; now you are the awareness, the conscious Presence that witnesses those states.[22]

Whether it's courage, faith, a touch of insanity, passion, or all of the above, some are propelled forward in the face of their fears; the benefits of living authentic lives and following passion outweigh the risks of following the guidance of their hearts. Whatever the guidance on the journeys, those fortunate enough to get to the punch line of the joke (in Tom Robbins's metaphor saying, life is the joke and the soul is the punch line of the joke) find their true calling. For lawyers, ego-driven and "in their heads" to start with, the path to authenticity, soul, and integration of the mind, body, heart, and soul can take many directions.

The paths of Rebecca Case-Grammatico and Dan Lindsey exemplify two such trailblazing endeavors. They both practice in legal services offices and represent low-income people who are in danger

---

22. Eckhart Tolle, *A New Earth: Awakening to Your Life's Purpose* (Penguin Group 2006), 117-118.

of losing their homes. Home ownership is a particularly valuable and irreplaceable asset for low-income families. Most of the clients these lawyers represent have been subject to unscrupulous, immoral lenders. The clients are in jeopardy of losing not only their homes, but also the hard-earned investments they have in their homes. Rebecca had one client who had to move temporarily after her son tragically died. The woman, who was taking care of her grand-daughter, entrusted her sister to pay the mortgage and taxes on her house while she was away for an extended period of time. Returning home, she found her house in foreclosure, her sister having ignored the responsibility to pay the bills. Relying on only her negotiating skills, as the client did not have any strong legal claims, Rebecca was able to save the woman's house. Not only that, the client ended up having a lower mortgage payment as Rebecca renegotiated her interest rate. In addition, Rebecca secured food stamps and health insurance for the client's granddaughter, a feat the client had been struggling to achieve.

Rebecca Case-Grammatico

Rebecca (Becky) Case-Grammatico's incredible energy and optimism is infectious. Her never-say-never attitude has carried her through a variety of difficult circumstances in her less than 30 years on this planet. In that same spirit, she is not daunted by the $100,000 of educational debt she accumulated from undergraduate school and law school loans, nor deterred from her commitment to public interest law, or in her words, "this lofty vision of change-the-world-type thing."

Becky originally planned on becoming a school teacher. While attending a Pennsylvania state school for teaching in Slippery Rock (north of Pittsburgh), one of her college professors convinced her that her exuberance and strength of conviction would be better served in a profession other than teaching. Becky decided to pursue a JD as a valuable avenue to accomplish the social change she desired. "I just knew that I intended to make a difference at some level," she says.

Becky set two requirements for her choice of law school: at least a "tier two" school and within a four-hour drive of her husband. Unaware of public interest law on entering law school, she did not seek out a school with a known public interest program. She had a vague idea that she would pursue family law, an area familiar to her from the custody battle her parents fought when she was a child. Becky soon discovered public interest law at Penn State Dickinson, where she attended law school. She remembers thinking, "Public interest was obviously the choice for what I wanted to pursue. I really wanted to have an impact on people's lives and use the law in a positive, productive manner."

Although most of the legal education at Dickinson was geared toward the world of corporate law and private practice, Becky aggressively tapped any public interest resources available. While looking into employment opportunities for the summer after her first year, Becky chanced upon a program at Dickinson that allowed students to work at a Legal Services office if they took an extra course on indigent law. Finding this program was a turning point for Becky, who recalls, "It was during that summer when I really understood that public interest was the avenue I wanted to pursue." Becky also had the good fortune of guidance from a professor who had been a legal services attorney in Georgia, Professor Michael Mogill. "He was a fabulous human being; a fabulous man whom I admired as a person, an attorney, and as a professor." Becky sought out advice from Professor Mogill about her public interest career. She was especially perplexed after hearing that the law school's Career Services office recommended that students eliminate all references to political affiliations from their résumés. Knowing that if she did so, there would be little, if anything, substantive left on her résumé, she sought out her mentor to confirm her gut feeling. "He said that because of my strong opinions and my strong beliefs, I probably wouldn't want to work for an employer that wouldn't hire me based on those affiliations. He suggested that I keep them in." Following her instincts and her wise advisor, Becky continued down the path on which her heart and soul had gently guided her.

Ever conscious of financial realities and her mounting debt, Becky worked two jobs during law school, a decrease from the two to three jobs she consistently worked during college. Despite her ever-growing commitment to public interest law, Becky had to accept a law clerk position at a personal injury law firm to help her pay her bills during law school. She labels the work on car accident litigation as "dreadful," but necessary to put food on the table. While employed at the private law firm, Becky also worked at the law school as an office assistant. She juggled both jobs with her studies until her third year when she became the managing editor of the International Law Review and had to cut back to one job. Because of the higher pay, she chose to keep the job at the personal injury firm. "It was the worst job though," she adds. Balancing her practical approach to earning money, which precipitated the brief foray into private practice during law school, Becky maintained an undying faith that things would work out financially. In deciding to go to law school she remembers reasoning that:

> I'm either going to do it or I'm not going to do it and I'm just going to have to bite the bullet and take the finances. I sort of figured that somehow it was going to be okay. I guess at that point my attitude was, I'll just figure it out and whatever it is, it is. I've never come from money by any stretch of the imagination so I just thought, "My parents never had much money and they somehow pulled through. I'll just do the same thing. I'll do what I need to do and that's the end of it."

Becky's persistence paid off while lobbying for a Loan Repayment Assistance Program (LRAP). When she first became a student there, Dickinson didn't have an LRAP. Becky started advocating for the LRAP the minute she decided to pursue a public interest law career. She credits "pure luck," but in reality it was her diligence, along with the help of two other law students, that established the institution of the LRAP two weeks before Becky graduated.

The five-year LRAP provides Becky with about $6,000 a year as long as she submits a renewal form every six months attesting to her continued public interest work and qualifying salary. The loan assistance makes a huge difference in budgeting her $37,000 annual salary with school loan payments of $600 a month added to her husband's school loans of $212 a month. Because her loans are over 25 and 30 years and the LRAP is for five years, she's enjoying it while she can.

Since graduating from Dickinson Law in 2003, Becky has worked at the Empire Justice Center in Rochester, New York, a public interest law firm, where she specializes in consumer law, specifically helping clients who have been prey to predatory mortgage lenders. She started at a salary of $32,500 and feels fortunate to have successfully competed for a highly sought-after position.

Her decision to move to upstate New York after law school, where her husband's family lives, was another leap of faith for Becky. She did not have the job yet at Empire Justice when she moved, but recalls, "I knew that something would come up and was confident that my résumé was strong enough to get me in somewhere." Continuing to reflect on that time of her life, Becky reflects:

> I made more connections in upstate New York than elsewhere and I had this phenomenal family unit that I was going to be married into. It seemed right and I just went with it, though it wasn't a comfortable jump of faith. It just felt like I had the support I needed and that I was somehow going to make it through. I was going to make it whether I was in New York or Pennsylvania or anywhere else. It wasn't a restful time period when I was trying to figure out what was going on with my life. I guess it was faith and just the support system that had been created all of a sudden around me.

The support Becky feels, tangible and believed, sustains her and her unfailing commitment to making the world a better place.

Her husband is a musician and she says, "His income is inconsistent." They have credit card debt from their school years. Becky has always been frugal with money and has never expected to enjoy a luxurious lifestyle. She and her husband were able to buy her husband's grandparents' house only by financing it through family. As she says, "I don't need the fancy clothes. I don't need the fancy car and I don't need the fancy house. We update one room in the house a year and even though we are still walking on the green shag carpet and looking at the outdated wood paneling that were left from Grandma and Grandpa, we're okay." The reason why Becky deals with the green shag carpet and the wood paneling is because "Every day I can look at myself in the mirror and be happy with myself and be happy with my life. I've got a wonderful family. I've got a great job that I enjoy coming to work to. My clients are phenomenal and I'm just happy, which is the best you can do, I think."

Given her own life and choices, Becky's advice for law students who want to remain focused on a public interest law career is predictable. Even with the $100,000 of debt she's still dealing with, she asserts:

> You can't let the debt overcome you. There's no real advice. Either you're going to do it or you're not going to do it. If you're going to do it then you'll find a way. You've found a way to get there so far and you just continue to do it. There's money out there. Look for it. There are offices out there that offer repayment programs. Either you want to do it or you don't and it's very clear to people. I think some people use the money as a crutch, as an excuse, frankly.

Becky's strong convictions and ability to be motivated by rewards other than money have kept her on the path of public interest lawyering. Although from a very different background than Becky, Dan Lindsey has found a similar path.

Dan Lindsey

Dan Lindsey's remarkable story is one of growing up in a well-to-do, supportive family in an affluent neighborhood, attending Harvard Law School, obtaining a coveted judicial clerkship after law school, and choosing, very deliberately, to adopt a simple lifestyle to do the public interest work he loves. He and his family have chosen a nontraditional path in their quest to make the world a better place. This quietly intense man with depth and wisdom glowing in his eyes has pictures of his three young children surrounding him in his office, so that he and his guests can gaze on them. It is evident where his priorities lie.

Dan's the one who, on very short notice and with little explanation, mobilized and arranged interviews with more attorneys at the Legal Assistance Foundation of Metropolitan Chicago than could be interviewed in the time I had allocated. His excitement at learning of my research project with the goal of inspiring potential lawyers to pursue public interest law was infectious throughout the legal services office. Public interest work is what he knew from the beginning he wanted to do. Answering the question, "How did you know?" his eyes glowing brighter, he explains:

> In my heart, mind, soul, deep inner being, whatever that was that inspired me to go to law school; made me want to go to law school. When you say it, it always sounds cliché, but I wanted to go to law school to help people. And I wanted to go to law school specifically to further, somewhere in the large description of justice, people who needed help, not just anybody who could afford a lawyer. I was just strongly motivated to get a law degree to serve, somehow, poor people, or people who were disadvantaged in some other way. I did do a lot of civil rights related work in law school, but probably I always had the focus on more economic issues,

economic justice or injustice. Looking back there's a fairly obvious trajectory, for me anyway, of doing civil legal services at the end of the day and helping people who are in poverty.

Dan identifies two interrelated motivating factors from his background. First is his strong religious belief system. Although no longer practicing the very conservative Southern Baptist faith he grew up in, Dan credits it as the beginning of a "religious, faith-based journey that led me to believe strongly that I had been given a lot and in return should look to use my gifts, my abilities, all the resources I've been given to help others. I saw that as I read the Bible and went to church. It became a stronger and stronger part of my personal faith journey." Describing it as his form of rebellion, Dan laughs when remembering how he read between the lines of the Bible and the sermons preached to find a faith-based commitment to economic justice. Today, his journey of faith continues, now with an Anabaptist Mennonite church where social justice and peace issues form a foundation of the belief system.

The second factor Dan credits for his steadfast commitment to using his privilege for the benefit of others is, ironically enough, growing up in a "lily white, affluent, conservative suburb with these huge homes and where everybody's rich." When Dan traveled to downtown Atlanta to go to a ballgame or other activity, he saw that "there are people on the other side of the economic divide and their lives and all the challenges are so dramatically different and there was just something wrong with the picture."

After graduating from Davidson, a small, liberal arts college north of Charlotte, North Carolina, Dan traveled far beyond downtown Atlanta to act on his desire to engage in economic justice work. His journey took him to Darfur, in the Sudan, where he performed relief work for more than a year with a group of Christian relief organizations. In the Sudan he experienced firsthand the incredible worldwide economic divide between the haves and the have-nots. Dan would apply to law schools from the Sudan. His year of relief work in the Sudan would lead him on his soul journey to law school.

Dan's parents helped support him through Harvard Law School. During that time, he married and his wife worked. Dan worked during summer breaks, one summer practicing at the Public Defender's Office and one summer at a private firm specifically to earn enough money to cover tuition. Even as early as the late 1980s, Harvard was supportive of students pursuing public interest law careers. It's developed even stronger support,[23] but Dan remembers that 10 percent of the students were dedicated to public interest careers, broadly defined. The school offered very strong clinical programs and faculty "icons," such as Professor Gary Bellow, as public-interest-minded role models. Harvard also has the Civil Rights/Civil Liberties Law Review and Dan became involved with it, ultimately serving as an editor. He remembers the "strong community of progressive people that was easy to find and be a part of since there was a large, minority, subculture of us, public interest types."

At the time of his graduation from Harvard Law School in 1990, Dan had accumulated about $10,000 in educational debt, a relatively low amount, due to the financial assistance he received from his parents and his wife's employment. Although he knew he would seek a public interest law position, Dan was not sure whether it would be in civil legal services or a position as a public defender. He decided to apply for federal judicial clerkships at the trial court level because he knew he wanted to litigate and knew a clerkship would be a great experience and help him decide. He received a two-year clerkship with a federal district court judge in Philadelphia. By the end of the two years, Dan was earning $62,000, a salary it would take him 15 years in legal services to attain again. In 1992, Dan started at the South Side neighborhood office of Legal Assistance Foundation in Chicago, at a salary of $36,000.

---

23. In March 2008, Harvard's support of students pursuing public interest law reached an all-time and unparalleled high when they announced that tuition for the third year of law school would be waived for all law students committing to public interest law work for years after law school. Jonathan D. Glater, "Harvard Law, Hoping Students Will Consider Public Service, Offers Tuition Break," New York Times, March 18, 2008, Education section, *available at* http://www.nytimes.com/2008/03/18/us/18law. html?ei=5124&en=201c22312730fa93&ex=1363579200&adxnnl=1&partner=permalink& exprod=permalink&adxnnlx=1205842535-Jja0vMpd7hTDlR9U11GRjQ.

After a few years in the neighborhood office, Dan was ready to take on more challenging and different cases than the two or three types of cases typical for the neighborhood practice. He applied for an opening in the downtown Chicago office but someone more senior got the job. Still not looking to leave legal services work, but wanting especially to do more complex litigation, Dan received a tempting call from a private firm that represented plaintiffs in consumer litigation. Dan remembers thinking, "It felt like I was still going to be doing public interest work even though it wasn't going to be a legal services organization. At the time it just seemed like the right thing to do. It was attractive enough to me to make the leap." Within a year's time, Dan realized that it wasn't a good fit. As he recalls, "I felt that, although some of our cases were on the side of the angels, it nonetheless was, on the bottom line, a profit, money-driven firm. It felt like I had strayed from the true public interest work that I had been called to do, or felt inspired to do. It just became increasingly clear that I wasn't cut out for that, so it wasn't the right place to be."

Dan left the private firm and worked for five years at the National Poverty Law Center in Chicago, practicing mostly housing law including, toward the end of his time there, predatory lending cases that were becoming prevalent in the late 1990s. When the position of supervising the Home Ownership Preservation Project at the Legal Assistance Foundation of Metropolitan Chicago opened up, he was ready to return to his home at legal services. Dan continues to hold this position, and at the time I spoke with him, he was supervising attorney for a special project that "represents homeowners who are threatened with the loss of their home either due to mortgage foreclosure, loss to a tax sale, sheriff sale, or increasingly, through various kinds of title fraud and foreclosure rescue fraud." The project Dan supervises also engages in policy work including collaborating "with the Attorney General to pass a new law in the state of Illinois targeting foreclosure rescue fraud. So we do work on the policy level . . . but our bread and butter work is representing individual clients."

Although raising three children on his public interest law salary, now at $72,500, and his wife's income from service work in job training, might be daunting for some, Dan shrugs off any hardship: "We just live a fairly modest lifestyle." They take public transportation, own only one car, and live in a fairly small duplex house that he and his wife bought with a friend. Dan reflects that "For me, there were economic trade-offs, but I hardly really even think of them as real trade-offs." He doesn't see them as trade-offs because:

> Although it hasn't been this way throughout my legal career, fortunately, in the last five years in this current position, I literally cannot imagine a job I'd much rather do. I literally love my job, at least most parts of it. There's junk with every job. Most days I really look forward to coming to work and the things I'm doing and the people I'm helping, it's just incredibly meaningful. It's also very challenging and intellectually stimulating. It's not just about helping; it's also meeting my creative and intellectual needs. Economically, obviously I made a lot of trade-offs but existentially how I experience my day every day I couldn't be in a better place.

Dan advises law students who want to follow the public interest law path to understand the lifestyle choices necessary to make it possible and to discipline themselves to live within their means. He believes that an important key to being able to maintain the necessary lifestyle is to find a community of supportive people with similar values. Dan's family has found such a community in his church, one "that very highly values simplicity of lifestyle and serving people and giving." Dan has also found that community at the office where he works. He says, "People are here to help each other and help our clients. We're not in competition or infighting, or politics. Okay, there's a little politics. On the whole, it's just a great community to be a part of."

Finally, Dan feels fortunate to have the support of his parents. His parents have never wanted for money and they are understanding and proud of their son's accomplishments and what motivates him. Dan says, "My parents are great. We disagree vehemently on many matters, political and otherwise, but they're very supportive and always have been." This support is, at times, ironic to Dan, considering his father's profession:

> It's funny, actually. Here I am sometimes suing finance companies and mortgage companies and lenders and my dad spent his entire life working his way up the rungs of General Electric Credit Corporation. They're actually, sometimes, defendants in our cases. So, it's like, "Thanks Dad, for all you did for me. I'm going to turn some of that back on your employer, the one who paid for my law school!"

His parents are proud of him, as are his children. The cycle continues.

B. THE WORK THEY LOVE

One of the many cases Dan has worked on in his years as a public interest lawyer was representing an elderly woman in her 70s whose primary source of income was Social Security, about $800 per month supplemented by about $700 a month she earned cleaning her neighbor's house. Dan describes her as "a sweet little old lady on the verge of senile dementia," barely making ends meet, when an unscrupulous mortgage broker talked her into borrowing money on a loan she could not afford. This elderly woman qualified for the loan only by virtue of the fact that the broker lied on her application, adding a "0" at the end of her monthly income so it read $7,000 a month. This is a true story, one of thousands contributing to this country's subprime mortgage lending crisis. The predatory lending institution immediately brought a foreclosure case against the woman's house when she could not meet even the first payment on her loan. Thankfully, she sought out the help of the legal services office and Dan defended her in the foreclosure action. Not only did he save her house, but he was also able to work out a settlement that included a reverse mortgage so that his client was guaranteed a roof over her head for the rest of her life.

Unscrupulous lenders in the subprime mortgage boom targeted low-income elderly and minority homeowners. Many public interest lawyers throughout the country are the only force standing between legitimate home ownership and certain foreclosure and homelessness at the hands of misleading and fraudulent predatory lenders. Becky Case remembers representing an African American couple who lived in their home taking care of six grandchildren. True to their practice of targeting minority homeowners, a lending institution, using unethical practices, talked the family into borrowing on the equity of their home. The terms the grandmother was promised on her loan and the terms she received were significantly different; her actual interest rate ended up being significantly higher than she was promised. Added to the misleading information, the lender secured a fraudulent home appraisal, doubling the value of the home, allowing a second mortgage to be hidden in the stack of paperwork at closing — which the client only found out about when she received two bills instead of one the first month of payments. Becky saved this home to eight people; she negotiated a reduction in interest rate on the first mortgage from 13 percent to 0 percent and eliminated the second mortgage. Becky calculates the client will save $220,847.39 over the life of the loans, in addition to keeping the home from foreclosure.

Legal services and legal aid attorneys such as Becky and Dan represent people who live in poverty in the United States. Poverty has been defined as "the state or condition of having little or no money, goods or means of support."[24] The U.S. Census Bureau defines being poor for one individual as an annual income of

---

24. http://dictionary.reference.com/browse/poverty

$10,294 or less. For a family of four it means living on less than $20,614 a year.[25] Poverty impacts women and children the most in our country. Almost 30 percent of female-headed households with no male present live in poverty and cannot maintain even that "minimum standard of well-being" for themselves and their children. The most conservative estimate for children living in poverty is about 18 percent of all children, but reliable estimates of child poverty in the United States go as high as 21.9 percent, the highest child poverty rate among developed nations. It's safe to say that about one in five children in the United States live in poverty. They are children living in the wealthiest nation in the world, yet exist in situations where there's not enough money to access adequate health care, live in decent housing, or buy nutritious food, let alone buy computers to attain the same level of education as those who have them, or manifest opportunities in life to break the cycle of poverty into which they were born.

The next story is that of Erin McCormack, an incredibly intelligent, dedicated, and hard-working attorney who graduated from law school in 2005. Erin currently practices law for the benefit of children living in poverty. She represents parents of children with disabilities, including one first grader she remembers who had a learning disability that caused him to have trouble learning to read and write. The struggle to learn was permeating his first grader experience, affecting him socially, and causing him to be withdrawn from his classmates. Erin was able to successfully represent the parents and guide them through the hearing process, which eventually forced the public school to provide the first grader with a tutor for the specialized instruction he needed.

Erin is especially proud of a case where she represented the parents of a teenager who has a learning disability along with

---

25. U.S. Census poverty figures, 2006.

emotional and physical disabilities. The New York City Department of Education had been providing home schooling of only one to two hours a day for four years, but the parents wanted an appropriate school placement. After the parents represented themselves at the impartial hearing, the Department of Education was ordered to find either a private or public school for the teenager to attend. When the parents were referred to the Partnership for Children's Rights where Erin works, a private school providing special education was identified for the teenager. For two years in a row, Erin battled to get the Department of Education to pay for the private school tuition because they had failed in providing an adequate public school education. For two years in a row, Erin has won.

Erin McCormack

Growing up in a family where community service and commitment to helping people were instilled as core values, Erin McCormack has known she'd devote herself to public interest work from a young age. From the time she was born, she has spent one week each summer at a camp run by her parents for children who are deaf. Erin's parents are both teachers and work at a school for deaf children in New York City, her father having been the principal, and now the director (formerly superintendent) of the school. When the school decided to start a camp in upstate New York and asked the McCormacks to be the volunteer managers of the camp, they agreed. They've been volunteering at the camp for more than 30 years. The school was founded by the Sisters of St. Joseph and they started the camp to give kids from low-income families an opportunity to leave the city in the summer. Erin reflects, "It's amazing to see their faces, to be out of the city. The kids don't get to go outside a lot, particularly since they're deaf and they can't communicate with the other kids. . . . They can't hear a car, they can't do a lot of things. They have the best time. It's just an incredible week for them." Erin is quick to add that the volunteer staff gets as much as, if not more, out of the experience than the children. "There are a lot of high school students who volunteer, who end up finding themselves, becoming teachers and going into special education; finding something that they didn't know they could do otherwise, that they could work with kids and make a difference."

It's no surprise that Erin has dedicated herself to public interest law and now works for the Partnership for Children's Rights (which changed its name from Legal Services for Children in January 2007) in Manhattan. Erin describes her work as follows:

> I represent low-income disabled children and their parents in seeking appropriate special education placements and services in administrative hearings against the New York City Department of Education and on appeal to the Office of State Review and the federal courts. I also represent low-income disabled children and their parents in appealing the denial of Supplemental Security Income (SSI) benefits in administrative proceedings before the Social Security Administration Office of Disability Adjudication and Review and on appeal to the federal courts.

Erin had a long-term plan from before she was in high school that included attending law school. She says, "I wish I could explain it in more objective terms, but it was just something I always knew I wanted to do. This is the way I could express the same thing that my parents do. It wasn't that I wanted to be a lawyer to be a lawyer. I thought that being a lawyer was the best way that I could serve the community." Erin's long-term plan included attending an undergraduate school where she could get a full scholarship. She did not want to have her choice of law school constrained by financial concerns so she based her undergraduate school decision on avoiding educational debt. Receiving a full scholarship from Fordham University made her decision easier. Her parents were able to pay the yearly room and board ($5,000–$8,000). Erin is conscious of the fact that it wasn't easy for them, especially because she has two younger siblings who also wanted to go to college, but she knows her choice was very important to them.

As in high school, Erin responded to opportunities to engage in community volunteer work in college. Fordham, being a Jesuit college, places a high priority on community service. Erin lived in the Bronx and became involved in the low-income community by doing after-school bilingual tutoring. She remembers that the first experience preceding orientation at Fordham was an "Urban Plunge" (an optional volunteer program before orientation started) where students get to know the community and perform volunteer work. It was important to Erin to be a positive force in the community for her four years there, "especially when colleges can be a negative part of the community." She remembers:

> I worked primarily with two boys at a Catholic school I was tutoring at and they were in seventh and eighth grades and their view of Fordham was very interesting. They said, "Oh, it's where they put up gates to keep us out." And it is gated and you don't think of that. But, of course, that's what it looks like to other people. It wasn't somewhere they could go ever, something to aspire to. It was something that was totally separate from their lives.

So Erin worked hard with the two boys beyond just tutoring to show them they could enter the gates and achieve whatever they set their minds to. She took them to campus events and showed them around and bought them Fordham T-shirts. In her words, "They didn't have the greatest starting point in life economically, and sometimes educationally, but I tried to inspire them and to be their advocate in a world that is not always tremendously friendly, especially if you're poor. It was something that was very important to me and something that I've been trying to carry with me into public interest law."

With her eye on the prize of a career in public interest law, Erin decided on New York University (NYU) for law school. NYU's commitment to public interest law and education is well-known. Erin knew of their LRAP and their financial support for students pursuing public interest law while in school, but when she visited the campus before deciding on a law school, she wanted to dig deeper and see what the overall and underlying attitudes were toward public interest work. She knew that many schools have a public interest "niche" that does not pervade the entire curriculum and faculty, but is focused on a small percentage of students committed to the work. Erin found what she was looking for at NYU. Even faculty and students who were not doing public interest work were very supportive of the public interest programs and people at NYU. Everyone Erin met, spoke to, and heard about were proud of NYU's reputation for devotion to public interest law. This commitment is evidenced by one of the most generous LRAPs in the country, summer stipends for public interest law internships, tuition scholarships, and a respect for social justice issues in the curriculum that is hard to surpass.

Despite her shared values and commitment to a public interest legal education, Erin found her colleagues at NYU initially intimidating. Many had gone to Ivy League undergraduate schools, were much older, or had been in the Peace Corps or begun their own nonprofit organizations. Erin received a valuable education at NYU in many ways, not the least of which was the lesson of self-acceptance, knowing she had a lot to contribute, and that "everyone brings something different to the table." Her law school career helped her define her uniqueness, guided by soul, and brought many opportunities to practice public interest law. She worked in the Brooklyn District Attorney's Office her first summer, which was "something really different," she admits with a laugh. Both her first summer's work and her second summer interning at Legal Services for Children were paid through NYU with public interest grants of $3,000 and $4,000 respectively. The DA's office wasn't really what she had envisioned doing but she learned a lot about legal research and writing that summer. The first day on the job she was handed a box and told "Here's your murder case," so it was good training in the trial-by-fire nature of public interest work. Erin enrolled in the criminal appellate defense clinic in law school where she learned a great deal. It was at Legal Services for Children, though, where she began work after law school graduation, that she found her passion.

She loved the client interaction and problem-solving nature of the hands-on work. Through her experience that second summer of law school she decided to apply for a Skadden Fellowship to work in the Legal Services for Children office after she graduated.

Erin received the Skadden Fellowship which is for two years. The first year her salary was $37,500. The second year the salary increased to $46,000. Making financial ends meet in New York City is possible because she lives in Queens and, due to good planning and living with her parents while attending law school, Erin was "only" $56,000 in educational debt when she graduated. Erin had received a partial scholarship of $10,000 a year for tuition, lived with her parents, and took the maximum amount of Stafford loans. She had also saved money throughout high school and college, working as a secretary in a law firm and from her law school summer jobs (the public interest grants from NYU). Erin confesses, "I'm not used to spending money. If you come from a family that has a ton of money, and you're used to shopping at expensive stores and doing things like that then I think it's much harder to adjust. My family is not poor but my parents are teachers so we're not rich either. I've always been used to shopping at Target and waiting 'til things go on sale. I don't go shopping a lot." And, she adds, "I think it keeps me a little more honest, in a way, not having a ton of money you still have to make good choices, and you remember how difficult it can be for other people, especially when that's the population you're working with. I think it's a little bit easier to relate when everything isn't easy for you too. I am aware of my clients' financial information because we have a financial cap and people support five children on less money than I make. So I know it can be done. That keeps it in perspective for me."

And, of course, the NYU LRAP has had a big impact on Erin's ability to live within her means on a public interest salary. She consolidated her loans and got a very good interest rate of about 2.6 percent fixed. On a 10-year payment plan her payments are $550 a month, which were totally covered by the LRAP her first Skadden year and mostly covered the second year. She knows her share of the payments will increase as she makes more money and, when she gets married to her longtime beau, her and her husband's salaries will be averaged and she might not qualify for the repayment assistance. When she first decided on NYU, the LRAP was a big factor in her choice, making her aware that the school concentrated its support on "preserving your choice to the end," as Erin remembers. "They're very intent on preserving people's choice so that they can go into public interest if that's what they want to do."

After life with the Skadden Fellowship, Erin knows she will continue with public interest law and stay in New York City. "I can't imagine doing anything but public interest law," she affirms. As she advises anyone pursuing a career in public interest law, "I think it's easier if you've made up your mind beforehand and say 'I'm going to stick to this,' rather than wavering in your mind. I think you need to know, in your heart and soul, you're just absolutely going to stick to it, and nothing's going to get in your way."

For her summer vacation this year, Erin volunteered again at the camp for deaf children. With a smile on her face she says, "That was the best vacation I could possibly have. Reminding me of why I do what I do."

C. LAWYERING FOR CONSTITUTIONAL RIGHTS

Families living in poverty cannot afford attorneys. When sources of income are jeopardized, when Medicaid or Medicare won't pay medical bills, when the utility company is threatening to shut off heat or electricity, when essential food stamps cannot be attained, people living in poverty cannot hire an attorney to fight for their subsistence. Nor can poor people afford to pay a lawyer to fight for their homes when they face foreclosure, or fight for their jobs when they've been fired — or not hired because of their race, or fight for access to adequate education for their children. Becky, Dan, and Erin work in comparatively low-paying lawyer jobs to be able to assist low-income people fighting for survival and their basic human and constitutional rights. Becky and Dan represent low-income families being threatened with homelessness by unscrupulous lenders out to make a profit at any cost. Erin represents children. Ben Elson, who works at the People's Law Office, a public interest law firm in Chicago, litigates cases where low-income people are being denied their constitutional rights.

Ben Elson

Ben Elson knows exactly what he wants to do in life and, despite his young years, has figured out how to do it. He graduated from law school in 2005 and has already embarked on a legal career enviable to the most seasoned lawyer. Ben's commitment to public interest law began at an early age. As he describes it:

> My commitment was driven by my radical politics which were shaped and influenced by my family, friends, community and education. I chose at an early age to identify with the people rather than with power and privilege. Growing up, I always felt a deep sympathy for people of color and their plight in this country.

Born into a family of lawyers, those values and the way to implement them in the world came naturally to Ben. His father died when he was four years old. According to Ben, "He was a man who was genuinely concerned with human suffering and its remedies and he used his law degree to represent the most vulnerable people amongst us, those less able to defend themselves because of their race or religion or age or mental condition." Ben was most influenced by his mother, whom he credits with his value system, and his uncle, his mother's brother, whom Ben is very close to. His uncle is a civil rights lawyer, author, radio host, political activist, and longtime National Lawyers Guild member in New York City. When Ben was a senior in high school, his uncle gave him William Kunstler's autobiography to read and it had a big impact on Ben, as one of those guideposts from soul along the journey.

In Ben's freshman year of undergraduate school at the University of Wisconsin in Madison, he had a clerkship with a Madison attorney named Mike Fox, who specialized in plaintiff's-side employment discrimination cases. The clerkship was a pivotal experience in Ben's life and it's when he decided he wanted to go to law school and become a civil rights attorney. He reflects that:

> I liked the way Mike used his legal skills and talents to help in the struggle of workers against their employers and the poor against the rich. I liked the type of people he represented and the impact he was making through his litigation. By successfully representing individuals whose rights had been violated, he was, in a way, merging his profession with movements of popular struggle.

Ben knew the limited financial prospects for the field of law he wanted to pursue so he continued at the University of Wisconsin for law school. It was the only law school he applied to, carrying on the family tradition, as his father and his uncle both graduated from the same state law school. Not only did Ben want to stay in Madison, which he loves, but also, for a top-tier law school, the tuition could not be beat at $10,000 a year. Ben financed law school with student loans and, even with the low tuition and help from his mom with living expenses, he graduated $55,000 in debt to the federal government. Having a best friend who graduated from Harvard Law School with $150,000 of debt puts it in perspective, though, for Ben. He considers himself lucky with payments of $250 a month over 20 years.

The debt load would have been greater had Ben not worked all throughout law school. After his first year of law school, Ben worked for a civil rights attorney in Madison named Jeff Scott Olson. He continued to work there throughout his second year of law school. The second summer Ben received a public interest law fellowship to work at the Center for Constitutional Rights in New York City, where, among other things, he worked on lawsuits filed on behalf of the detainees at Guantanamo Bay, Cuba, who had been deprived of their right to challenge their detention in court. The $2,000 stipend was for the entire summer, so Ben lived with his uncle in New York City to do the work he wanted to do. Back in Madison for his third year of law school, Ben continued to work for Jeff Scott Olson. Ben loved the work and remembers:

> I barely went to class because I was so interested in working on Jeff's cases. He was a sole practitioner with hundreds of cases and since I was his only law clerk, he gave me a tremendous amount of responsibility. I spent approximately 25 hours a week during law school working for him, which you're not supposed to do, but I did anyway because I believed the practical experience I was receiving from him was far more important than the case law I was memorizing in law school.

After graduating from law school, Ben was intent on finding a job that would give him a chance to continue to live his values; salary was not a major consideration. "I knew the type of law I wanted to practice and I was looking for a firm that fit my politics and values. Salary took a back seat to these considerations." Ben found his dream job at the People's Law Office in Chicago, a for-profit, public interest law firm that handles a spectrum of civil rights cases. Ben's youthful and straight-laced appearance cast doubt on the stereotypical image of a social justice lawyer. Explaining the cases he's working on give even shorter life to those doubts:

> I'm involved in complex civil litigation against the City of Chicago surrounding the Jon Burge police torture scandal that started in the early '70s and continued through the early '90s. My firm filed wrongful conviction cases on behalf of two men who were tortured by Burge and his men into falsely confessing to murders they did not commit and spent many years in prison until they were eventually exonerated. After they were both exonerated, my office filed wrongful

conviction lawsuits against the City of Chicago and the police officers who tortured them into giving false confessions. I'm also involved in an extremely important and high-profile criminal defense case of a Palestinian-born American citizen who was indicted by John Ashcroft for allegedly providing material support to Hamas. In addition to those cases, I have several police misconduct cases which I'm primarily responsible for with limited supervision from the partners in my office.

The excitement Ben exhibits for his work is unique among first-year associates. He beams while explaining, "For the first time in my life, I can't wait to get to work in the morning." And, further, "I want to do the best I can for my clients because I genuinely care for them and their struggles." The $40,000 annual salary he earns meets his criteria of making ends meet, as long as he lives frugally and simply. As Ben explains:

Almost my entire paycheck goes toward paying rent, groceries, and my student loans. I don't have a car payment and public transportation in Chicago is relatively cheap and easy. You don't have to make $100,000 a year to live comfortably in this city. While I may not be accumulating money in my savings account, the psychic income I receive from my work is far more valuable.

With his love of his job, Ben has no regrets, reflecting, "I know how lucky I am to have this job. Very few people have the opportunity to get paid to do what they love and believe in." From the stories Ben has heard about people graduating from law school, taking a big firm job, and hating it, he knows there's a huge contrast between his life and theirs. "You really don't hear stories like that from people who take public interest jobs. For the most part, they love the work they're doing."

Ben doesn't understand why more lawyers don't practice in the public interest. His parting words are:

> We're at a crucial moment in this country's history. erosion of the rule of law and the dramatic cutbacks in our civil rights that have occurred under the guise of fighting terrorism have brought about the most sustained and deepest assault on liberty that we have ever seen. It's disappointing that so few law school graduates can find it in themselves to forego the big paycheck in favor of using their skills to struggle against the power structure. The obligation for lawyers who truly want to do good work is to resist the Bush administration's attempt to take us down a path of lawlessness.

This is emphatically stated by a young, passionate man with his whole career in front of him.

D. LAWYERING FOR SYSTEMIC SOLUTIONS TO POVERTY

Public interest lawyers have always been in the forefront of the struggle for equality, fairness, justice, and the right of every human being to have the opportunity for well-being and respect. The founding principles of our country, borne out of a deep desire to end oppression and construct a form of governance based on fairness and equality, aimed to ensure human rights. As these principles have eroded in practice, and been challenged, long ago in our country's history and very recently, at the hands of men intent on maintaining power over other human beings, it has been public interest lawyers who rally to the aid of people denied their fundamental human rights. Public interest lawyers have fought for individual rights, civil rights, and the right of every person to a minimum means of subsistence. When our federal and state governments began to reduce assistance for low-income people, and to diminish the rights of poor, disabled, and elderly people to even the most minimum standard of living, public interest lawyers fought hard and continue to fight on behalf of the people being denied their survival needs. When the federal government proved ineffective in combating the effects of poverty on low-income neighborhoods, public interest lawyers got creative in their legal representation of individuals and communities. Lawyering for social change took on a new significance in the years following the severe government cutbacks of the 1980s that eliminated or drastically reduced funding for programs to revitalize communities where low-income people live. The not-for-profit sector began to step in where government programs abandoned the people in those communities. Public interest lawyers were called on to devise legal mechanisms and strategies to foster economic growth where there was little hope of opportunity. The community economic development movement, as it would be called, was created by public interest lawyers and others as a response to government policies benefitting the rich with the senseless and empty hope that somehow the bounty would "trickle down" to the poor. What has happened, through the determination of social change lawyers and the community organizations and individuals they represent, is slow but lasting economic growth from within low-income communities. What has occurred is a systemic approach to the problem of poverty, accompanied by an education and empowerment of people to creatively address the causes of poverty to better their own lives. What has occurred is a collective effort to transform communities house by house, block by block, and business by business. What has happened is that the collective heart and soul of communities, with the assistance of social change lawyers, have brought about community revitalization unparalleled in our nation's history.

One of the founders of community economic development, now a revered elder of the movement, is Paul Acinapura, a wise, creative, incredibly resourceful man who was called to public interest lawyering and who remains overwhelmingly passionate about the work he does. Susan Chase and Jessica Rose are the next generation of community economic development attorneys. Susan works at Legal Aid in Manhattan practicing community development law. Jessie Rose sought out Paul Acinapura to work with him, knowing the cutting edge work he still accomplishes for low-income communities, and because of her deep desire to bring economic justice to low-income communities. Their stories serve as examples of public interest lawyers called to use their legal skills for positive social change, improving the lives of whole communities of people.

Paul Acinapura

Paul Acinapura has a twinkle in his blue eyes that would rival Polaris, even at twilight. He's 60 years of age (give or take a couple years) and he graduated from law school in 1973. The quintessential legal services attorney, Paul has worked in legal services since graduating. The job he now has at the Brooklyn Legal Services Corporation A (East Brooklyn) office was the first job he got out of law school. The social turmoil of the 1960s led Paul on the path to public interest law. Although he doesn't remember exactly what his motivation was, he does remember "some sense of wanting to make a contribution and wanting to serve and assist in some way." He had attended NYU for undergraduate school and then did graduate work in communications at the University of Pennsylvania. In between graduate school and law school, Paul worked for a few newspapers and as an assistant film editor for a media company.

When he decided to attend law school, Paul knew he wanted to stay on the East Coast and he applied to NYU and Rutgers University in Newark, New Jersey. He was accepted at both law schools but his New Jersey residency created a tuition differential of $4,000, as Rutgers would cost him $500 a year and NYU would cost $4,500 a year. Economically, the choice was clear. He remembers:

> I knew I was going to do public interest work and I think it was, "Well, I can get a good legal education where the tuition, when all is said and done, will be $1,500 as opposed to, I'll get a good legal education

and my debt will be $14,000." I guess there is a tie-in because I knew when I finished I was going to do public interest work so I guess in some way I must have thought, "Well I'm going to be doing public interest work. I'm not going to be practicing law for purposes of making whatever huge salary would have been then. Since I'm going to be working in that sector, and I'm not going to be working for purposes of a huge salary, and I am going to have debt, I should keep my debt low."

Paul's debt on graduation 30 years ago was $4,500, a lot of money for the time. Working through law school helped pay living expenses. Paul had work-study funding and was able to work in the law school clinic. Rutgers had become one of the first law schools in the country to have a fairly large clinic. Paul also worked as a research assistant to one of the professors. So when he graduated and started work at Brooklyn Legal Services Corporation A at an annual salary of $10,500, his lifestyle did not change all that much. He was living with three other people (two public interest lawyers and one freelance artist) and they were able to live comfortably. As Paul says, "I was a young kid in my mid-20s. I had worked through college, I worked through graduate school, I had scuffled about in the years between graduate school and law school and I worked through law school. I felt I was maintaining the same sort of student, comfortable living style. I didn't feel crimped at all." The loan payments he had of $127 monthly over a ten-year period were doable even at his public interest salary.

Although significantly higher than the $10,500 annual salary Paul started at more than 30 thirty years ago, he knows his salary now is significantly less than the starting salary of law school graduates at Wall Street firms. Paul is General Counsel and Managing Attorney of Brooklyn Legal Services Corporation A and he heads the community economic development unit, earning $105,000 a year. Married since about five years out of law school, Paul and his wife have two grown sons. His wife worked all the years they were raising their sons so they've always had a two-income household. For 20 years, Paul's wife had her own catering business and for almost 15 years she's been the program coordinator at Columbia University's graduate school of public health. They've maintained what Paul characterizes as a "simple lifestyle" and when asked whether there have been any trade-offs, Paul answers thoughtfully:

> Well, I don't think so. I mean, here is why I said no. Trade-off seems to indicate that, for example "Well I want to have a house in the Hamptons but I can't have a house in the Hamptons because I work in the public interest." Or, "I want to spend two months a year in France but I can't because I have a public interest salary." When I think about a trade-off, that's not my life. Those would not be my choices. I don't feel that I've had to make trade-offs. There are probably points in time in my life where a little more salary into the household would have felt better and maybe made things more easily addressed. But I don't feel they were trade-offs.

Not feeling that he's sacrificed to pursue the work he loves, the rewards are all the richer. Paul reflects that the work "speaks to who I am and touches my core values. It's rewarding on many different levels." In fact, Paul can be uncharacteristically emotive about his work, saying:

> I'm in love with it. I have a number of clients with whom I work who are religiously affiliated and connected both in the work that they do and in their other parts of life. I notice on occasion, because these are clients and friends for 25 or 30 years, so I notice on occasion some of their language has slipped into my head and, on occasion, I've used the phrase that I'll use now. I actually feel *blessed* that I have been able to find a place to do this work.

Equally as blessed are Paul's clients. To say that Paul is a pioneer in the field of community economic development (CED) law is an understatement. This area of law, currently considered cutting edge, has been the work that Paul has been passionately in love with for 30 years. He is a father of the CED movement, creatively applying traditional legal skills in nontraditional ways to positively impact and improve the lives of low-income people and the neighborhoods in which they live. Hired to practice landlord-tenant law, Paul worked full-time in landlord-tenant court for two years. He also began representing tenant associations and, unlike many legal services attorneys in similar positions, Paul would be responsive when clients asked him to think outside the box about their legal needs. Most of the questions would be generated by clients on boards of community organizations or church social action committees regarding, for example, a lease for a day care center or a real estate transaction involving a shelter for victims of domestic violence. In 1976, as Paul's practice of law expanded to accommodate the legal needs of his clients, Paul convinced his then managing attorney to allow him to represent community organizations full-time, an unprecedented move in legal services practice nationwide. Now, his practice includes representation of community organizations involved in affordable housing development, the creation and operation of day care centers, senior citizen centers, and health care centers. In some cases, Paul has been house counsel to the community-based organizations for more than 30 years. Of the importance of CED work to the low-income communities he represents, Paul says:

> It's actually an area of practice that ought to be, *ought to be* an element of core practice for any public interest law practice that identifies itself as committed to neighborhoods and to a neighborhood base. Because it empowers communities, it helps to empower neighborhoods, it helps to empower people, oppressed from racial or economic, class, or race reasons, or some combination of both. What it does is it empowers individuals, communities, and

families to take control of their future, take control of
their lives, take control of forces which historically
have engaged in benign neglect or affirmative
oppression and enables them to stand up and to
move their future in a positive way defined by themselves and *that*, to me, *that* is part and parcel of what
the war on poverty was about. I mean, that was our
birth mother, so to speak, of Legal Services and public
interest law practice, was to give communities the
tools in their own hands to define their future,
meet their needs, and serve the needs of their grand-
mothers, and their mothers and their fathers, and
their children.

Talking about the work he's in love with, the twinkle in Paul's
eyes could light up the D train, standing motionless in a tunnel of the
New York City subway system during a blackout. The twinkle continues to glow while pondering advice for law school graduates
nowadays wanting to follow this time-honored path. He starts by
saying, "I guess my first comment would be stay true to your commitment, and stay true to what you want to do. That is the easy thing
to say but I mean that." His next piece of advice recalls the discus-
sion about trade-offs. Although Paul doesn't feel his work has
demanded any great sacrifice in terms of lifestyle, he knows that
currently the low wages for public interest attorneys and the amount
of debt from law school might very well require significant trade-
offs. Recognizing that such trade-offs are inevitable would be a good
idea from the start so that when they do happen "you can say to
yourself 'ha ha . . . I knew it . . . I knew this would happen!' so that
it doesn't come as a surprise." And then the ultimate wisdom from
this elder of the legal services community:

If you want to do public interest law and make a
choice after law school that you're not going to do
it because of your debt and you are going to do
something else so that you have a higher salary to

address your debt, well, you made a trade-off there, didn't you? So you're ultimately making *another* trade-off and the trade-off that you're making in that context is doing something that you don't really want to do to pay your debt. And then you're working really, not because of your commitment and your dedication and your philosophy, but you're working for the financial institution, no matter who your employer is, you are working for the people that hold your loan and that's a trade-off.

Knowing himself, his commitment, his core values, and his dedication to public interest law, Paul can look back on his 30-plus years as a lawyer and sum it up smiling: "I'm middle-aged, I'm Caucasian, I'm bald and I'm passionate about my work. I hope it's part of my being. It is part of my being."

Susan Chase

Susan Chase received a degree in microbiology before deciding to enroll in law school. Always having an affinity for math and science, and as a minority student possessing that affinity, she was pushed in that direction. After working at places like Los Alamos National Laboratories and doing cancer research at Sloan Kettering Hospital, Susan decided work as a scientist was not what she wanted to do in life. When she pondered what it was that she liked doing, rather than what was expected of her, it didn't take her long to realize what she really wanted to do was work in the community and organize people to improve their own lives and neighborhoods. Susan had done a lot of work in the community in high school and she says, "I could do it *very well.* I could bring people together and I could motivate them toward a cause." Susan applied to law school thinking she would pursue a career in public interest law; she knew she was deeply interested in social change and social justice issues.

Growing up in Macon, Georgia, Susan saw firsthand the lack of opportunity for poor people. "There's really a vast difference if you've got money or if you don't," she reflects. At a young age she became interested in neighborhood revitalization and affordable housing development, seeing the deterioration of the neighborhood she grew up in and in which her family continues to live. Later on, while she was in law school, Susan worked with her mother to get funding to renovate and certify a historic home in the neighborhood. It was frustrating to Susan that no one else in the neighborhood undertook a similar endeavor that could have transformed the community.

Susan exudes wisdom and maturity beyond her years. That wisdom held her in good stead in deciding to attend a law school that would be the least expensive of her options. Knowing she would probably go into public interest law, she chose to go to the University of Texas at Austin where her costs would be half that of most New York City schools. Instead of pursuing similarly ranked schools in New York City, she decided to attend the University of Texas, thinking, "Why not go there and get the same high-quality education for half the money?" Still, Susan graduated with over $70,000 of educational debt, $65,000 from law school and $8,000 from undergraduate school at Howard University. And, in case life wasn't exciting and challenging enough, Susan was married during her second year of law school to someone she'd known for six years. They had their first of three children during Susan's third year of law school.

Thank goodness Susan has unbounded energy. Her high energy and enthusiastic intensity were evident throughout her interview, despite the fact she confessed she was having a "bad" day, having worked until 9:00 p.m. every night that week. We met on a Friday. One wonders what a good day might be like, knowing the incredible energy Susan exhibits on a bad day.

It took Susan a couple of years after graduating from law school to realize her dream of working at the Legal Aid Society of New York. She applied right out of law school, in 1994, but that was a year of turmoil for Legal Aid, as then-Mayor Giuliani cancelled the attorneys' contracts after a strike was called and consequently caused a hiring freeze. Susan's application and résumé were kept on file and a position opened in 1996, which she took. In the meantime, she was home with her baby and did some contract work for a small, civil law practice. Starting at the Bronx Legal Aid office practicing housing law, mostly eviction prevention, Susan remembers two clients in particular who had a great impact on her. Both were women, one of whom annoyed Susan at first. Susan admits having adopted a not-so-flattering name for the client, who Susan teased behind her back for annoying behavior. The woman was facing eviction for nonpayment of rent. One day Susan understood that the client actually had the mental capacity of a 12-year-old and Susan's heart went out to her for the problems her mental capacity issues had caused her. She had never been given any assistance for her disabilities, had never gotten any help. The client couldn't do even simple math and so had been giving her boyfriend the money she made to pay the rent. He had not been paying the rent for her, but had been pocketing the money, so she was facing eviction. Through the course of representing her, Susan discovered that the woman had an uncle who cared about her but did not know the trouble she was in. Susan was able to arrange for the uncle to become representative payee for the client, responsibly paying her bills, and preventing the eviction. But Susan didn't stop there. Bringing a social worker in to work on the case, they were able to enroll the client in a math class and, the last Susan knew, the woman was able to write her own checks. It was a humbling experience for Susan, a lesson in not judging and about the danger of making assumptions about people.

Susan's dedication to providing opportunities to people who wouldn't otherwise have anywhere to turn prevailed through her representation of a woman with a psychiatric disorder. This client thought people were stealing food from her apartment, so she traveled everywhere with a cart filled with her food. The client was especially hard to deal with, but Susan found inner strength and patience — even when the client would yell at her, thinking Susan was someone in her life who was actually dead. This woman was also facing eviction and Susan is sure that she would have been homeless if not for the legal assistance. Even though mentally challenged, the client's sole source of income was public assistance. Susan immediately helped her apply for Social Security disability income and guided her through the process, even personally intervening when the employees at the Social Security office became exasperated with the client. Without bragging, Susan relates that the client would have been on the street but for the legal services provided.

After working in both the Bronx and Brooklyn offices on private housing and federally subsidized housing issues for the tenant/owners, Susan now works on the Community Development Project of the Housing Development Unit in the Harlem office. The attorneys in the Housing Development Unit consider the Community Development Project so important that they're willing to take on an overload of cases to be able to allocate three attorneys to the Community Development Project.

When Susan began at Legal Aid in 1996 her salary was about $34,000 annually. At that time, her husband was a school teacher and his salary was comparable to hers. Lance worked two jobs and he would take opportunities to teach after school so they could make their financial ends meet. Slowly, their finances have improved. Susan's salary jumped to $50,000 when she transferred to the Harlem office in 2001. Lance earned his master's degree and his salary increased. But, with three children born in the span of five years starting in Susan's last year of law school, the family has always been on a tight budget. After ten years at Legal Aid, Susan is earning less than $90,000. The family watches every penny. A high priority has always been saving money. "I'm a very good saver," Susan states proudly. "I look at raises as opportunities to put away money and, every time that I've gotten a raise after my first year I've saved. I started with putting away $25. I would put most, if not all, of my raise into my retirement fund. My check now doesn't look much different than my check when I was making half of what I do now."

To be able to save for retirement and support a family of five in the Manhattan area, Susan maintains awareness of their fiscal limitations, including:

> I don't eat out a lot. I take my lunch to work. I'm still
> very frugal about grocery shopping and about going

out, although sometimes I don't want to be. I'd love
to have a subscription to Lincoln Center, which we
did, when we didn't have kids. On vacations, we usually drive where we go. I'd love to send my kids to a
really nice camp but we don't. Our kids go to the "Y."
We believe in public schools. We were very lucky
when we found our home. We were blessed because
we got the property when it was vacant and, in the
middle of winter, the seller wanted to get rid of it. We
probably couldn't afford our house now.

They pay less in mortgage payments than they would for rent.
They also just bought their first new car because her husband opens
the high school he works at and he has to be there on time. The
family usually drives to their vacation destinations, although they
did travel inexpensively to Ecuador in 2001. Susan loves to travel, so
when the opportunity presented itself to stay at a friend's apartment,
she grabbed it. There's an account on her computer for retirement
savings and one for saving for travel. Susan says "I'm a saver. I think
in order to do this kind of work you have to know how to live off of
this kind of money. I've never had money before. You know, in my
young life, my mother was a working person, but she could stretch a
dollar. And I think it's hard if you don't know how to stretch a dollar.
And sometimes it's disappointing. I mean, it's not like I don't want to
do certain things. I've had to say to my friends, 'You know, I can't. I
can't fly to Jamaica for an anniversary party, or I can't go with you
here.' You know. There are things that I want for my kids that I can't
do." When asked why the work is so important that she's willing to
make those trade-offs, she quickly replies, "You know what? I *enjoy*
it. Most of the time I feel like I'm making change. Most of the
time. You know I'm not going to waste my life doing something
I don't like doing."

This committed wife, mother, and public interest lawyer has
sage advice for anyone wanting to make public interest law a career.
She begins with knowing how to manage debt from the beginning;
taking a hard look at how you're spending money while in law

school after choosing a law school based on low cost or a good LRAP. Susan emphasizes, "You have to be really disciplined and you *have* to budget. Law school debt is good debt." Once working in public interest law, "You have to pay yourself first. There is no reason why you should be broke working a public interest job." It's also important to consolidate loans and get on a modified or graduated payment plan, even if it's spread out over 30 years. "Then as you make more money, target it to paying off more of the debt." And, Susan cannot stress enough, "Just because you don't make much money doesn't mean not to save. You must, you must pay yourself first. It's very crucial that you have an emergency fund." Finally, Susan reflects on the innate wisdom that if you're doing good work, the work you love "you are going to make money at it. You can write a book (laughs). And it will come. If you do what you're passionate about, what you love, no matter what it is, the money will come."

Jessica Rose

By her own admission, Jessie Rose has always kept her "eye on the prize." Jessie was born into a family of generations of political activists and considers public interest law and work her "natural disposition." After graduating from college with a major in sociology and a minor in Latin American and Caribbean area studies, she returned to New York City and worked for a Puerto Rican youth agency called ASPIRA of New York, Inc. The experience convinced her to attend law school because:

> I was doing youth development and youth organizing work and I was doing some other community organizing work on my own time. I worked with a number of young people who were undocumented immigrants. Even though the organization started as a Puerto Rican youth agency it opened its doors to the growing Latino population and I was frustrated at the lack of options for higher education that the

undocumented students were facing. And, I was frus-
trated at my own limitations as an organizer because
the law didn't work in their favor; there wasn't actually that much that we could do. So, I started thinking
about legal advocacy.

A deliberate planner, Jessie by temperament always deliberately and consciously plans her next steps in life. Jessie decided
she needed some experience in the legal field before making the
commitment (not the least of which was financial) to law school.
She went to work as a paralegal for the Legal Aid Society, working
for a year in the Brooklyn office doing housing and government
benefits work. She then worked for a year in the citywide immigration unit. The two years gave her the certainty and knowledge that
she indeed wanted to be a lawyer. Jessie enrolled at Fordham
University School of Law, knowing that she wanted to pursue social
change lawyering and become a public interest lawyer.

In law school, Jessie "naturally gravitated toward public
interest-minded students and faculty." Fordham has the Stein
Scholars Program for Ethics and Public Interest Law and Jessie
found a home in that program. She took special public interest
courses and worked in the public interest law area during the
summer. The Stein Scholars is a competitive program that Jessie
applied for in her second year of law school. Only four or five
second-year law students are chosen every year and Jessie was
one of them (the majority of Stein Scholars apply as incoming
first-year law students). Through her participation in the Stein
program, she came to know the public interest professors, many
of whom had been legal aid attorneys in New York City. Receiving
a $2,000 public interest stipend, Jessie worked at the Center for
Constitutional Rights during her first summer of law school.

In her third year of law school, Jessie enrolled in the CED clinic,
supervised by a former legal services attorney in his first year of
teaching the clinic. She was inspired and guided to the work she

grew passionate about. Very quickly she realized that CED work was her calling. In Jessie's words:

> I had realized that more and more I liked transactional work as opposed to litigation work. It fit into my political orientation in terms of using law to make institutional change. That was my real frustration with some of the work I had done at Legal Aid. You're preventing evictions but you're not solving the problem that people fundamentally can't afford the houses they're living in. You help a small part of the immigration process but the larger construct of the immigration laws is not changing. So, I was frustrated at a lot of the shortcomings of some of the representation. Not a shortcoming of the lawyers who do the work. It's just a shortcoming of the entire legal structure. So, it was through the clinic that I realized what kind of work I wanted to do.

The one obstacle between Jessie's desire to enter the public interest law arena after law school and her ability to do so was the fact that she graduated from law school $160,000 in educational debt. All of Jessie's debt was from law school. She had no debt from undergraduate education because she attended the State University of New York at Binghamton and her parents were able to help her out with the state tuition. The financial aid counselor Jessie spoke with her first year of law school warned her that every $1,000 of private debt matters. Having borrowed the maximum amount of federally subsidized loans, Jessie still needed $60,000 in private loans to meet the high tuition costs at Fordham, and to live (even inexpensively) in New York City. The financial aid counselor had told her to rework her budget and think about not giving holiday and birthday gifts for a few years. Although Jessie did trim her budget and didn't give extravagant gifts, the joy she receives from gift-giving overrode her need for frugality. With $160,000 in debt (the private loan portion of which carried a very high interest rate). Jessie could not see her way clear to work for a public interest law salary after graduating law school. During her second summer of law school, Jessie had worked for a public finance law firm, had been paid a summer associate's salary, and had enjoyed the work. Knowing that she ultimately wanted to be a public interest lawyer, she made the difficult decision to work at the firm after graduation as a way of paying off her debt more quickly.

Jessie's determination and ability to "keep an eye on the prize" served her well during the three years she worked at the law firm. As opposed to almost every law student who envisions themselves a public interest lawyer but gets detoured by the lure of sizable salaries in the private sector, Jessie maintained a standard of living more fitting a public interest lawyer while she was earning about $100,000 a year at the firm. The salary seemed "an absurd amount of money except for the fact that I was working 50 to 70 hours a week. I was working two full-time jobs. So, if you think about it that way, it's not that absurd." Luckily, Jessie was able to consolidate her Stafford loans at a 4 percent interest rate and she immediately began overpaying her monthly payments.

She remembers the time clearly:

> So, in the three years at the firm I just continued to live at the same level that I was living at. The problem is when you go into a firm and you get seduced by the high pay. And, also, you're working so hard, and you're so tired, and you feel like you deserve to say, "Oh, I'll take my friends out for dinner because I haven't seen them in two months." Or, "I have 4 days off, I'm gonna go and do some luxurious little vacation," or whatever. But, if you control yourself and you have, not a frugal life, but just control your budget, you know, I was able to put everything away. My entire bonus every year went straight to the student loans. So, in three years I paid $100,000 off.

That's not a typo. In three years, Jessie paid $100,000 of her student loans. One might even call it "soulful budgeting!"

The firm had also given Jessie the ability to get her feet wet practicing transactional law. Jessie was an associate in a group that was primarily bond counsel and underwriting counsel to public entities such as the Metropolitan Transit Authority and the Environmental Facilities Corporation. From Jessie's perspective,

> I was lucky because I knew that I wanted to do CED work. I was very clear in terms of the kind of public interest work that I wanted to do after graduation. So, when I realized for me, I was most comfortable getting a job to help me pay off a significant amount for a few years, I was lucky to have found the firm that I worked with which was transactional work within the public framework. My skills were really translatable to this practice. It wasn't three years of lost time. I was getting the skills needed to do this kind of work.

Through the extended network of the Stein Scholars Program and clinical program at Fordham, Jessie was able to continue her connections with the public interest law world so "it's not like you're totally divorced and it's just some other reality." Jessie had known about the work in Community Economic Development ongoing at Brooklyn Legal Services Corporation A from her clinic professor. She had approached the Executive Director, Paul Acinapura, to explore applying for fellowships for postgraduate funding for a staff position. As those discussions were progressing, one of the staff attorneys decided to leave and Jessie decided to apply for the job; a job that was the exact job she wanted. Focused on paying off her educational debt, Jessie could not commit to her heart's desire until she resolved in her mind that it was okay to still be almost $60,000 in debt. She remembers thinking:

> It was a little bit sooner than I had anticipated because I hadn't been able to pay off the full loan.

61

> I looked around and I don't know many lawyers. Most
> of my friends are social workers, teachers, and
> nonprofit workers. So, I said, "Their average masters
> degree is about $50,000." You know, my sister, who
> works in a nonprofit, my friend who's a therapist, and
> they're all doing community work, and they're all
> being able to manage. They pay their rent. They're
> able to do this. I said, "I can make the jump now. I can
> go back to public interest because now the debt is to
> an amount that I can actually live with." So, that's
> what I've been doing. But, it's been tight, budget-
> wise because Legal Services doesn't pay that much
> money.

Now in her sixth year of practicing law, Jessie earns $49,000 a
year. She was able to buy her first apartment but only because she
had a little savings from the private sector job and because she lives
with her twin sister and they help each other out. When Jessie was
working at the firm, she would take her sister on vacation. Recently,
they had to travel for family reasons and her sister bought Jessie's
plane ticket. Financially, it's tight but she reasons that "I can absolutely live. I can afford my apartment. I can afford food and cloth-
ing." What Jessie can't afford are vacations every year and a car and
car insurance. But, she says:

> It's totally doable and I'm much happier than I was at
> the firm. I'm doing what I believe in. It's what I always
> wanted to do. I'm fulfilled professionally. I love the
> people I work with. I love my clients. I think, psychi-
> cally, it's easier to work diligently and hard when you
> really believe in what you're doing and you love the
> people you're working with.

The work Jessie loves doing is in the Community Economic
Development Unit of Brooklyn Legal Services Corporation A. Her
areas of representation include affordable housing development,

development of a facility for a health care center, and facilities development for a school. About 85 percent of the work she does involves financing for real estate and facility development, but she also represents some not-for-profit organizations incorporating and applying for tax-exempt status (and other nonprofit corporate matters) and then continues to advise them as in-house counsel. When asked if she can envision doing this work forever she replies:

> Yes. More so than not. I really love the work that I'm doing, and I feel good about it when I wake up in the morning and I just get so much out of it. So on one level I can see myself doing it for a very long time; certainly CED work for a long time, I don't know, policy work also interests me, teaching also interests me. I'm single and at some point I want a family so I don't know how that would factor into it. This office is pretty open and supportive to those kinds of changes in somebody's life. You never know.

Jessie considers herself lucky. She has a job she loves and she has the support of her family and friends. Making the jump from the firm to legal services and the more than 50 percent pay cut would have been a lot harder for her were it not for her family believing in her and believing in the work. "They're all supportive of it. They see how I'm happier. They were scared for me to make the financial jump but I got a lot of support in my decision."

For others embarking on the public interest law path, Jessie counsels: "If you can minimize the amount of private debt that you take out . . . that's key." The role of law schools in counseling first-year students spiraling down into that debt is also key; realistically explaining how it will impact life and its options. Jessie says:

> And, honestly, I have counseled many people who've thought about going to law school and I've told them "You really need to think about this because it is a

tremendous amount of money." You don't want to go into it in two years and just say "I hate the law, I don't want to do this" because it's too late and you owe a lot of money and you're going to have to pay it back. The best advice I give is before you make the decision to go to law school . . . do it because you know you want to do it. When you get out, you've just bought a luxury house . . . and you don't have a house to live in (laughs). But, you have the skills, you have a degree that you really wanted and you're not going to regret it.

Jessie would not dissuade anyone from pursuing a dream of being a public interest lawyer. Yes, find ways to avoid private debt. Get roommates. Take off a year or two between college and law school to save money. Live with your parents if you have to, but the bottom line is, "I mean — it really sounds really hokey — but I feel like if you really want to do it you can. It's not without its difficulties but everything has its pros and cons." Jessie's matter-of-fact, hello-to-life attitude provokes one last incredibly shiny pearl of wisdom that can only be stated verbatim:

In the larger scheme of things . . . let's get real. We live in a country where everything is based on debt. You ALWAYS are going to be in debt if you live in the United States (big laugh). You buy a house, you're in debt. You buy a car, you're in debt. You have children and you send them for private education, you're in debt. You're always going to be in debt. Part of it for me is, "Oh my god, I have $100,000 debt already paid off" (yeah!), pay it off and you're going to have another debt. You've got to accept that part of that is living in a society that we live in. And, unfortunately, that's just the reality of it. People have educational debt. That's just the reality nowadays.

E. CONCLUSION

Job satisfaction can be a truly elusive phenomenon nowadays. Most people, let alone, most attorneys, do not have rewarding jobs they look forward to working at during their long laboring days. To find work that is fulfilling and stays true to our most authentic selves is an incredible gift. For those who listen to their internal guidance and follow their hearts and souls, passion for work is attainable. Some people know all along what they are passionate about and the work that will fulfill them. Some are certain that the passion they carry will propel them to do something meaningful to help others. Some find guideposts along the way or are mentored by someone who helps point them in the right direction. Listening to that deep inner voice, not letting fear silence it, following your heart and your passion, whatever it might be, can lead to a career path destined to be rewarding. Listening to the voice of the heart and not allowing monetary concerns to be the guiding force allows us to experience the true benefits of not sacrificing authenticity. Finding support systems along the path, from family, friends, organized religion, and colleagues at the office is essential.

The public interest lawyers interviewed for this book all love their jobs. The financial sacrifices they make to work at jobs they love are insignificant compared to the emotional, spiritual, and psychological sacrifices necessary if they did not stay true to their values. As we've seen, though, there are many obstacles on the path of attaining authenticity. Actually, those obstacles represent one of the ways we can be sure we're on a road paved by our hearts and souls, testing our determination, exercising our strength of character, and bringing us closer to the depths of our being.

We turn now to the obstacles.

CHAPTER 4

Embracing the Challenges and Obstacles

A. LAW SCHOOL AND THE PURSUIT OF PUBLIC INTEREST LAW

Law school can harden the heart and be hard on the soul. The emphasis on legal analysis and logical problem solving is undoubtedly necessary but can create psychic imbalances when presented to the exclusion of heartfelt and soul-centered approaches to lawyering. Third-year law students have had few, if any, opportunities to exercise any of the tangible and intangible muscles they were born with, except their brain muscles. Learning to feel and create as lawyers comes much harder to most law students than learning to think like lawyers. By the time they are third-year law students and the analytical method of legal reasoning is drummed into their brains to the exclusion of any other method of problem solving, feeling and creating are viewed as forces to be controlled rather than nurtured. There are, however, innovative and creative law professors and programs, changing legal education and the legal profession. Depending on the law school and the law student's ability to see beyond the mainstream, by the third year, students can be exposed to creative ways of approaching lawyering in addition to the analytical approach.

At the beginning of the academic year, I tell my third-year law students entering the Community Development Law Clinic that I expect their entire person to show up for the clinic. When I speak of an approach to lawyering that integrates mind, heart, and soul, they mostly look at me as if my hair is on fire. When I speak of the whole person as lawyer, needing to accept that we have emotions, feelings, and creative instincts that influence our lawyering, they are sure that I deliberately set the fire that is now raging around my head.

Passion often is viewed as a suspect force to be relegated to one's personal life and not allowed to cross the line into one's professional life. Legal education (as with most professional education) has a lot to learn about mind, heart, and soul integration. Social psychology explains that reason and emotion must both be present for human intelligence to operate.[26] As the Dalai Lama says, "The proper utilization of our intelligence and knowledge is to effect changes from within to develop a good heart."[27] To excel as a lawyer, what researchers have called "multiple intelligences" must be practiced, honed as skills, and utilized.[28] To be the best we can be in any discipline or aspect of our lives, we have to draw on all facets of intelligence and the totality of the mind, body, and soul, and, of course, heart connection we so often ignore.

For law students, becoming lawyers who draw on all aspects of themselves to lawyer the best they can is a challenge in and of itself.

---

26. Jonathan Haidt, *The Happiness Hypothesis: Finding Modern Truth in Ancient Wisdom* (Basic Books 2006), 13.

27. Dalai Lama, *The Art of Happiness: A Handbook for Living* (Riverhead 1998), 52.

28. Howard Gardner, *Multiple Intelligences: New Horizons* (Basic Books 2006), 4.

To stay true to a heart-centered, passionate calling of becoming a lawyer to help society's most disadvantaged people is often a monumental task in today's prevailing system of legal education. Legal education not only focuses primarily on the mind to the detriment of all other problem solving and creative aspects of a person, it also focuses primarily on lawyering for people and corporations that have money, and money-related status quo legal problems most prevalent among the middle and upper classes and among for-profit corporations.[29] Most law schools do not support the pursuit of public interest law and, through lack of encouragement, dissuade law students who have that original goal from achieving it. The fires of passion and the passionate pursuit of public interest law are easily smothered. Most law students, drained of their idealism and quest for social justice by the time they graduate, deny their passion for justice, take the path most traveled, and end up with legal jobs in the private sector. It is only the bravest and most determined that continue on the path less traveled, propelled by an inner motivation and undeterred by the lack of external support. Hasan Shafiqullah is one such person.

Hasan represents people diagnosed with HIV/AIDS. One of his clients is a man who had to quit his job due to his illness. He was facing eviction because he couldn't pay his rent. Hasan advocated for the client with the New York City HIV/AIDS Service Administration, and the client qualified for cash assistance, food stamps, and further, the advocacy led to the City paying his rent every month, in addition to paying the rent arrears. Without Hasan's assistance, the client would have faced loss of his apartment at a time in his life

---

29. Many commentators observe this imbalance of emphasis in law school: David C. Vladeck, "Hard Choices: Thoughts for New Lawyers," 10 *Kan Journal of Law & Public Policy* 351 (2001); William P. Quigley, "Letter to a Law Student Interested in Social Justice," 1 *DePaul Journal for Social Justice* 7 (Fall 2007); Kimberly McKelvey, "Public Interest Lawyering in the United States and Montana: Past, Present and Future," 67 *Montana Law Review* 377 (Summer 2006); Jessica Davis, "Social Justice and Legal Education: Mandatory Pro Bono Legal Services," 1 *Charleston L. Rev.* 85 (Fall 2006); Amy Bradshaw, "Exploring Law Students' Attitudes, Beliefs, and Experiences About the Relationship Between Business Law and Public Interest Law," 20 *Wisconsin Women's Law Journal* 287 (Fall 2005): 292; Patrick J. Schlitz, *supra* note 15.

when he needed to spend his energy on fighting a life-threatening disease.

Hasan also represents people who are actively dying of AIDS, such as a woman with two children, who needed legal help appointing a guardian to care for her children after her death. Hasan drafted a standby guardianship designation and, after the client's death, helped the guardian through the process of obtaining guardianship from Family Court.

Hasan Shafiqullah

Hasan Shafiqullah was born in Canada, where his parents emigrated from Bangladesh in 1961. When he was ten months old, the family moved to Tucson, Arizona, where he grew up. There are two defining characteristics that Hasan credits for his nontraditional lifestyle and commitment to public interest law. The first is his country of origin. Hasan has journeyed to Bangladesh a handful of times and reflects on his evolving perspective of his roots:

> My mother is one of 15 kids and my father is one of 11, so I have a ton of cousins and second cousins in Bangladesh. It's sobering knowing that many of them live in poverty and that very few of them made it out of the country. I'm very aware of my privilege and of how amazing it is for me to be living here and to have all these resources at my disposal. When I went to Bangladesh for the first time I was 7 years old and was appalled by the poverty. I was a horrible, spoiled little Western child and kept saying that I wanted to go back to Tucson, that Bangladesh was a country of beggars. I went again in 1986, when I was 17. I really connected to the people that time and felt that it was my country. The last time was 1994 and I was 25 years old and just loved it. It was amazing to be in a place where everyone looked like me; there was a real feeling of homecoming. Still, the poverty

was overwhelming. We really aren't aware of just how
privileged we are here in the West.

Despite Hasan's awareness of his privilege, he is also aware that
the color of his skin gives him an "outsider perspective on society."
This perspective stems also from the fact that he's gay and was a
cross-dresser for many years. It's made him realize that "I'd never be
happy or never would remotely fit in, in a corporate culture. But
also, beyond just fitting in, the outsider status spoke to me more and
so doing public interest work was sort of a natural fit for me."

Hasan initially majored in classical music in college, attending
the University of Arizona at Tucson, where both of his parents
worked. He had played the cello for 11 years. After three years as
a cellist in undergraduate school, his cello professor "told me that
I had no talent, and that I should look for another career, and I think
he was right. I didn't really have the talent to make it profession-
ally." Uncertain where his interests lie aside from the cello, Hasan
studied a broad liberal arts curriculum. He finally found inspiration,
a guidepost, and direction when Ralph Nader spoke on campus
about using law for social change. Hasan's previous impression of
law as merely ambulance chasing was expanded, as was his major.
He developed a prelaw major comprised of a triple minor in anthro-
pology, East Asian studies and a mixture of political science and
humanities. Because his parents worked at the university (his father
as a research scientist, his mother in administration), his tuition was
only $150 a semester, and he lived at home, so it didn't matter much
financially that Hasan took six years to finish undergraduate school.

At the age of 19, Hasan had come out to his parents as gay. He
describes it as "a huge thing," having grown up in a very strict
Islamic household, remembering:

> My father had founded the Mosque in Tucson in 1970
> and he was one of the cornerstones of the Islamic
> community there, he and my mother both, and he
> was the Muslim students' advisor for the campus
> and the President of the Mosque for a couple of

decades. When I came out I was in the LGBT group on campus and there was much, much conflict between him and me. All that sort of radicalized me, and I ended up becoming very militantly gay. When I was in Washington, DC, I was arrested in front of the White House protesting the ban on gays and lesbians in the military. The arrest was on CNN. Even on campus in undergrad, before going to DC, I was involved in protests and all that sort of work. So, queer consciousness, and person of color consciousness and racial justice work, all that was interesting to me and it was along those lines that I wanted to work eventually.

Part of Hasan's undergraduate education included a trip to Washington, DC, in 1993 to intern with the United States Student Association's Lesbian, Gay, Bisexual, Transgender Caucus and the People of Color Caucus. While there, he got involved with the Campaign for Military Service, a coalition group fighting the exclusion of gays from the military. Deciding to move to San Francisco later that year, Hasan then took a year off from school, working as a pathology assistant doing autopsies and studying for the LSAT.

He applied to New York University, Northeastern School of Law, and the University of California at Hastings School of Law in San Francisco. He did not get into NYU, but did get accepted by Hastings and Northeastern. By then he could go to Hastings on in-state tuition, so he stayed in California. The tuition he paid at Hastings was $14,000 a year. If he had gone to law school at the University of Arizona and lived with his parents he would have graduated debt-free, as the tuition would have been $150 per semester, as both of his parents worked there. As it turned out, his desire to live away from home led him to graduate with a law school debt load of $55,000. Hasan credits his frugal lifestyle with keeping his living expenses, and thereby his debt, low. Throughout law school he lived in a two-and-a-half-bedroom apartment in San Francisco with two other people. The apartment was rent-stabilized, so in Hasan's words, "My rent was insanely low; I was paying $350, I think."

All of his living expenses were paid for by the money he borrowed for law school because the work that Hasan did in law school was mostly volunteering. He did have work-study funding that paid very little for his work in the law library his second year of law school. During the first summer he received a small student stipend for being a research assistant for a professor and the second summer he volunteered as a law clerk at the ACLU Northern California office. His entire second year of law school, Hasan clerked at the National Center for Lesbian Rights, also for no pay.

Hastings did not feel very public-interest friendly to Hasan. He remembers that "it seemed like a place for corporate practitioners for the most part. It seemed like the public interest people were in the substantial minority." This environment led Hasan to feel very alienated, to the point that he recalls, "Those were the three most unhappy years of my life. I was deeply miserable and I had to create my own little world and find my own mentors. There was this group of radical dykes who had been admitted the year before me who were my support network there. They sort of got me through and they got me involved in the clinical program, which I did for two years." He knows it has changed now but, in the mid-1990s when he was attending law school, the clinical programs were marginalized. Hasan worked in the housing rights clinic and then with the San Francisco Human Rights Commission, working on adopting regulations with a lesbian, gay, bisexual, and transgendered youth task force. This experience and "the leftist students in the clinics got me through the law school experience."

Despite the marginalization of public interest law at Hastings, the work experiences that Hasan sought and maintained convinced him of his desire to pursue public interest law. "I really wanted to do public interest type work, but I wasn't sure where I wanted to head. I wasn't sure I even wanted to take the bar exam. I wasn't sure what I was doing at this point," Hasan remembers. A friend of Hasan's had been working for a tenants' rights attorney and referred him for the job. Hasan ended up taking the California bar and really enjoying the housing and eviction defense work he did for the solo practitioner. Although he was working in a private practice, Hasan very much considered himself to be doing public interest law, working on tenants' rights cases in San Francisco and earning $35,000 a year, as well as volunteering at the San Francisco Tenant's Union one night a week. The for-profit status of the firm, though, made him ineligible for the Hastings LRAP. Two years after graduating law school, and after passing the New York and New Jersey bars, Hasan moved to New York City (in July 1999) and got a job at Queens Legal Services, with a starting salary of $37,000. After his nine-month deferral ran out, his monthly loan payments were $650. Hasan remembers that he didn't go out much because his rent in the apartment he shared was $720. Between rent and school loan payments, there weren't any discretionary funds. For a few months, Hasan even had a second job as a waiter on weekends just to make ends meet. Then, after he had been practicing at Legal Services for a year, he became eligible for LRAP, but after about three years, his salary increased to more than the $40,000 maximum for the loan repayment assistance. Hasan had been living in the East Village for eight months when he first moved to New York City and then found a cheaper apartment in Jersey City for two years. His rent was about $575 a month in New Jersey but, after September 11, 2001, the commute from Jersey City into Queens became too difficult (all the commuters who had taken the PATH train from New Jersey into Manhattan through the World Trade Center were now squeezed on to the other PATH line), so he moved to Brooklyn. Of his residence now he says, "I live in a very small studio, less than 250 square feet in a poor neighborhood in Brooklyn, in Flatbush. My rent is only $550 a month, and because the rent is so low I've been able to aggressively pay down my student loans." For the first time in his adult life, Hasan has no roommates, saying, "I was so tired of roommates."

Hasan's frugal lifestyle and inexpensive living arrangements have given him the opportunity to not only pay his student loans (he paid the $55,000 off in August 2005, only eight years after graduating, even with three deferrals), but also to start a small retirement fund and to indulge his love of travel. Since June 2001, Hasan has been working at the Legal Aid Society's Harlem office, in the

HIV/AIDS Representation Project, providing a broad range of legal services to people who are HIV positive. He describes his practice as:

> They have to be HIV positive to get in the door but what I do isn't necessarily related to their HIV status. I do mostly housing eviction defense cases and some family law, government benefits, welfare, social security or SSI, and a lot of wills and health care proxies. Also, stand-by guardianship designations for people who are care-takers of minor children and who have a terminal illness, HIV or cancer. I also handle credit issues, and I've been doing transgender name changes . . . and anything else that comes in the door.

Once Hasan's salary increased into the $50,000 range, he began to travel. He has an incredible poster-sized photograph in his office of him hang-gliding in Brazil. That was in 2004. He's spent ten days in Spain and took a month off to live in Paris. He has traveled to France five times. He's been to Costa Rica and Acapulco and Greece. So, he says, "I'm having a good life as a public interest attorney," and he explains how he's able to do it:

> I've been able to take the vacations I have because I live very cheaply and have low rent. Brazil cost me about $1,200 out of pocket. Spain was $1,500. Costa Rica was $1,500. The trick is to earn frequent flyer miles. Brazil was on frequent flyer miles, Spain was on a free ticket — they had this deal that if you flew twice in the U.S. on American or Delta, you get a free ticket anywhere in the world that those airlines fly. So, I got a $134 ticket to San Francisco and a $170 ticket to Miami and that got me a free ticket to Spain. Costa Rica was free on frequent flyer. Acapulco was a free ticket (the airline had mistakenly offered it for $0, which I learned about on flyertalk.com and booked before they caught the error, about a 30-minute window of opportunity)

and Greece was free on frequent flyer. The thing is to book your mileage flights at least nine months in advance, since there are so few mileage seats available per flight. Of course, if I hadn't been taking these vacations I would have been done paying off my loans much sooner, but I have no regrets.

Due to the salary steps at Legal Aid, Hasan is earning about $76,000 now, but in the New York City area he's on a tight budget to pay bills, save for travel, and save a little for retirement. This tight budget includes bringing his lunch to work every day, finding inexpensive restaurants when he does eat out, such as a Trinidadian fast food place near his apartment in Brooklyn where he can buy dinner for $5. He sees shows, but only for $3 a seat purchased through audienceextras.com the day of, or the day before, the performance. He emphasizes that he doesn't buy a lot of consumer goods.

Part of Hasan's inspiration is a friend he looks at as a role model:

One of my touchstones for all of this is a friend of mine in San Francisco who's 45 now. When he was going through his undergrad he was planning to be a professor. All of his friends went on to teach at Berkeley and he was going to do that as well, but early on he decided he didn't want to be part of all that so he just, sort of, dropped out of the whole grind. He's worked in a used bookstore for the last 25 years; lives in an SRO hotel in San Francisco for $250 a month; and is actually saving a little money. He lives this monk-like existence. He has no furnishings, just some thin carpets, a little hot plate, no fridge, and some chimes hanging on the walls and that's it. And one little bookshelf. He's totally happy and it's all he needs. Every time I think "Oh, I should really move into a bigger apartment" or I should really upgrade this way or that way, I think about him and ask myself how much is really necessary to be happy?

> So, I keep pulling back from efforts to upgrade my
> lifestyle to something more luxurious or expensive.

It helps that Hasan "loves" his work. He says, "What keeps me motivated is I love what I do. I love the clients that I work with, for the most part. It feels like I'm making a huge difference in people's daily lives, so that part I really like. That's what keeps me going." Hasan knows he could be making a lot more money in the corporate world, but to him the work he does is the reward. When asked if he could do it forever, he answers:

> I love this kind of work. I do need a break from liti-
> gating, but I think I'm just getting tired after nine
> years. So, actually next year I'm taking a leave of
> absence from Legal Aid; under our union contract
> we can take a leave for up to 12 months and be
> guaranteed our position back. To prepare for that,
> so that I'll have money to support myself for a year,
> I'm currently getting certified as a French translator
> through NYU and will hopefully be translating legal
> documents in Paris and Montreal next year.

When he returns from the year abroad, Hasan plans to start saving aggressively for retirement. He plans to continue to live inexpensively because "I have $26,000 saved up for retirement, which is totally inadequate for a 37-year-old. I should have much more than $26,000 at this point."

This rare gem of a person and public interest lawyer, a soft-spoken, sensitive man with a depth of character and integrity obvious even on first impression, has very rare, practical advice for others. First, he counsels to "agitate" for a loan forgiveness program at the law school of your choice, if one doesn't already exist. And, he says to make sure "the disbursements are given as cancelable loans, not as cash grants, because under Internal Revenue Code sec. 108(f) if it's given as a cancelable loan it's not taxable, but if it's a cash grant it is taxable." (After graduating, he organized a group of alums who convinced Hastings to switch from cash grants to cancelable loans.) His final piece of advice comes from the heart: "Find a community of public interest minded people. I think if you plug into it, it will make it much easier to not lose sight of public interest after you graduate." Nor do you have to lose sight of a dream to hang glide over Rio de Janeiro some day.

B. FINDING THE PASSION DESPITE THE OBSTACLES

Hasan found a comfortable place in an otherwise uncomfortable environment by connecting with like-minded people. He stayed true to his desire of pursuing public interest law because of the support from other law students wanting to do the same. This approach has been promoted by researchers and writers studying the obstacles faced by law students intent on maintaining public interest career goals. As noted by Carrie Menkel-Meadow, writing about "cause lawyering" and reflecting on the work of Robert Stover at the University of Denver Law School:

> Interestingly, Stover suggests that those who were successful in maintaining their public interest commitment were able to do so by forming support groups and immersing themselves in a public interest "subculture" in response to the dominant culture of law school, perhaps demonstrating the importance of the "network" in maintaining altruistic actions and motivations.[30]

---

30. Carrie Menkel-Meadow, "The Causes of Cause Lawyering: Toward an Understanding of the Motivation and Commitment of Social Justice Lawyers," in *Cause Lawyering: Political Commitments and Professional Responsibilities*, by Austin Sarat and Stuart A. Scheingold (Oxford University Press 1998). *See also* Michael J. Steinberg, "Why I Chose Public Service Over Private Practice," 85 *Michigan Bar Journal* 28 (June 2006) reporting in footnote 2 that "A core group of students active in the National Lawyers Guild supported each other's political and career interests during law school."

Crystal Doody found a program and professors in law school that sparked her interest and guided her on the public interest path she chose. She is one of the rare exceptions to the rule that law school deadens passion and her story proves that law students can become passionate about helping others during law school, despite the odds. Having found that passion, Crystal is now doing her work from her heart, representing people with disabilities. Crystal helps children with disabilities stay in school and helps people with mental illness avoid institutionalization. She represented one ten-year-old boy who has Tourette syndrome with a serious side effect of severe anxiety, causing him to miss many days at school. Despite the fact that his disability was well documented to the school by his many medical providers, the school filed a PINS ("People in Need of Supervision") petition in court against the child, claiming truancy and excessive absences. Crystal was able to get the petition dismissed by the court and obtained a signed agreement by the school district saying they would not pursue a PINS petition again. As with most public interest lawyers, Crystal is determined to be proactive, not just reactive, and is pursuing special education services for the boy that he is entitled to under the law.

Crystal also represents a woman with a severe mental illness who is able to maintain her own apartment and remain in her familiar community because of help she receives a few hours a day cleaning and cooking. Without Crystal's intervention, the client was threatened with denial of the services she depended on.

Crystal Doody

Crystal Doody's parents knew the value of an education, but also knew they couldn't afford to send Crystal and her three siblings to college. Her father is a parts manager at a car dealership and her mom was an extremely involved stay-at-home mom while the kids were growing up and now works part time. Getting good grades was a high priority in the family and Crystal remembers being in big trouble if she came home with a bad report card. The only higher education that Crystal knew was within her reach was community college and she reflects, "Community college was expected of me, but beyond that, it kind of stopped there. It wasn't even discussed because we couldn't afford it." Her parents didn't know the possibilities for financing an education. And, because the family had moved to a middle-class suburb from the city of Rochester when Crystal was in the fifth grade and her parents inherited her grandfather's house, the high school guidance counselors assumed that all the students would go to college and that their parents could afford it. Crystal would finally meet someone who would take the time to explain the options to her when she was enrolled in community college. The mentor Crystal met, Holly, was a returning student at the community college and they met through the honors program at the school. Holly was surprised that Crystal was not continuing on after graduating from the two-year criminal justice program she was in and, when she found out the reason, detailed for Crystal all the scholarships, grants, loans, and work-study funding available.

After her world was "opened up," Crystal went on to the State University of New York at Albany to graduate with a bachelor's degree from a four-year school. Having lived with her parents during the two years of community college and then going to a state school for two years and working all through undergraduate school, sometimes 25 to 32 hours a week during the school year in addition to full-time work in the summers, Crystal was able to limit the amount of money she borrowed for undergraduate school. The debt she incurred during that time was $10,000. She remembers, "When I moved out and moved to Albany I had to support myself and pay my rent and student loans weren't going to do it and I didn't take very much out at all for personal expenses in student loans during my undergrad. I was working overnights from 11:00 p.m. to 7:00 a.m. with people with disabilities and I'd go to class and I'd go home."

The only time in her life Crystal remembers not working is when she was studying for the New York State bar exam, after graduating law school. She took two years off after graduating from college and worked as a claims examiner for an insurance company. The reason she waited to go to law school was "I wanted to go right from college to law school but I really had my heart set on Syracuse and I got wait-listed. So, I decided to retake the LSAT because that was where my weakness was and then I got in two years later." Deciding to go to law school during community college, Crystal knew that she would go to graduate school but mostly knew what she didn't want to do. As she explains:

> It wasn't really that I knew that I wanted to be a law-yer, it was that I knew a lot of things that I didn't want to do and I knew that I could do something with a law degree and it would be meaningful in some way. I really hadn't defined it much more than that until I got to law school. I was going to law school without a realistic idea of what career options there were available to me. I figured that I'd figure it out in law school.

It's hard reviewing Crystal's journey without using an obvious wordplay with her name, as the clarity that occurred in community college ended up repeating itself in law school (in other words, it became Crystal clear). Crystal's faith in being able to "figure it out" as she went along bore results her very first semester of law school. Dedicated to getting as much education as possible, Crystal read her first Career Services newsletter and paid great attention to the joint degree programs Syracuse University offers. None of them sparked her interest until she began to read about a new joint degree being offered between the College of Law and the School of Education in disability studies. Having worked nights through undergraduate school in a residence for people with disabilities she had some background and she says, "It just seemed like the perfect joint degree to do." The program in disability studies would shape Crystal's legal education and her career, and it brought her into contact with a tight-knit group of students and a supportive faculty who she describes as "so passionate that it was absolutely conta-gious." She continues:

> I think it's pretty unique and really, what's extra special about it is that it's literally a handful of people.

If I hadn't gotten in with that handful of people I could have ended up anywhere because I was really open to doing almost anything and it could have been in any area within Syracuse Law that I could have gotten wrapped up in and that just happened to be the one. There was, literally, probably three faculty members, one being from the law school, two from the school of education and maybe three other students at the law school, and that tiny group of people motivated me to the point where I had a really wonderful track to go off of.

That track would land Crystal a position handling disability rights cases at Legal Services of Central New York within a year of graduating from law school in May 2005. The cases involve employment discrimination, special education, and a wide variety of legal issues for people who are disabled. The love of the disabilities studies program in law school has definitely translated into the love of the practice of disability law for Crystal. As she replies when asked why she loves the work:

I think it's twofold. First of all, it's the kind of work that I do, the clients that I'm serving. There aren't enough people doing the work. It's so desperately needed. The disability rights perspective is so very important to me personally. It's a population that is perceived as being helpless and childlike and all these different things that absolutely irritate me and to be able to back people up in the things they're trying to do in their everyday lives is so important. I just absolutely love the work that I do. Helping kids with disabilities get accommodations in school and get services they need in fourth grade because the school districts are saying they don't have the money to give them speech therapy and all these different things is just so incredibly important.

And the other half of it is working for an organization like this gives me the flexibility in my job that I think working in the private sector would not give me. We work a lot of hours depending on what our cases are like. We rarely turn away cases because it's so hard for us to do that. In our blood we hate doing that and so we only turn away cases when there isn't a case. Where there are just no legal grounds to say there's a case. But if there's a case we take it, so we generally have heavy caseloads and they run the gamut from one area of practice all the way to another so you have to learn something new all the time, which is great.

Crystal's enthusiasm and passion for her work do not dwindle when she starts to talk about her educational debt from law school. Added to the $10,000 from undergraduate was almost $142,000 in loans from law school, even though she avoided the living expenses of New York City by deliberately going to law school in upstate New York. The knowledge that someday she'd be paying about $1,000 a month in school loan payments occurred to Crystal in law school but did not deter her. "It was absolutely not something that was going to change my mind," she says, but it was something that she tried to control. Law school was no exception to her working her way through school and she babysat at least 15 to 20 hours a week at $10 an hour. She details how she managed the work and school:

I left criminal law class ten minutes early each day, with permission, so I could get the littlest one and go pick her up from school and be home in time to get the other two off the bus. And I'd get dinner, and do homework and baths and put them to bed and then was free from 8:00 p.m. on. It was a few days a week and I loved it. What was great was that I was able to frame my schoolwork and do my schoolwork and

I was able to find things that worked with my
schedule and paid me.

The summer after her first year of law school, Crystal took
classes and babysat. The second summer she had a work-study
position at Legal Services. She tried to cut costs during law school
to keep her debt as low as possible, finding apartments with inexpensive rent and roommates with whom to split the rent. "I'm
always, always, always, trying to find a cheap way to do things.
I've always been like that," she says. With her starting salary of
$32,250 (slightly higher than the $31,000 starting salary because
she also has a master's degree) at Legal Services, which recently
increased to $33,750, Crystal worries what will happen after a
temporary reprieve from the more than $1,000 monthly loan pay-
ments she faces. Her payments now are $660 a month during the
reprieve.[31]

The financial worries Crystal experiences are somewhat alle-
viated by the fact that she has found a part-time job two evenings
a week at a local two-year for-profit college, teaching criminal justice, critical thinking, and business law. She earns about $10,800
a year, depending on how many courses she teaches, which is a
sizeable amount to Crystal. When she decided to try to buy a house,
she qualified for a $70,000 mortgage. This is a finite amount by any
standards, but Crystal knew she'd be able to find a house in Syracuse, New York, within that price range. As it turned out, she
found an old arts and crafts bungalow being foreclosed and was
able to purchase it for $46,000. The neighborhood might be
referred to as transitional because it borders a very low-income

---

31. As an update, Crystal worries about the impact of the new federal loan forgiveness program on her monthly payment amount. Half of her loans are private and have a
9 percent interest rate. In 2008, her payments on the federal and private loans were $1,100
per month without the forgiveness program. Ironically, with the federal loan forgiveness
program, her payments would be $1,300 a month for the ten-year repayment period.
Although ultimately she will benefit after the ten-year repayment period and will most
likely save approximately $30,000, her current problem is acute.

and a middle-income neighborhood, but Crystal and her partner love it. She says:

> It is absolutely gorgeous. It had a new roof, it had a new furnace. All the essential parts of the house were in fabulous shape. The trim needed to be painted and the rooms needed to be painted and it needed to be cleaned on the inside because someone had lived there for a long time and it was just a little dirty. It had beautiful hardwood floors, a stone fireplace; all those great things. It was foreclosed so happened to be a great deal.

Despite taking all the financially wise steps, finding a house to buy where she's paying less in monthly mortgage payments than she was in rent, and working two jobs, Crystal is counting on a sizeable salary increase to be able to stay at Legal Services once her school loan payments increase to over $1,000 a month. She's hopeful the attorney's union will negotiate a salary scale that is more favorable to the newer attorneys this year. When asked if she would consider going to a job in the private sector if the salary increase doesn't happen, Crystal replies:

> It is the absolute last thing on earth that I want to do; I don't honestly know if I could. I just don't know if I could give up this kind of a job to do anything else. And if I did something else I don't know if I would go into the private sector. What I think I would do instead is look into disability rights jobs where I could be doing the sort of work that I do now, maybe not quite as wonderful. I wouldn't be able to have this job but I would be able to do disability rights work maybe in a government sector or I could do disability stuff for a college or something like that.

As the salary negotiations continue, Crystal continues to love her job and is passionate about the work she does. She says,

"This office in particular is amazing. I love the people I work with. The attorneys who I see myself as twenty years from now work here and they're just phenomenal." Crystal loves the people in the office and she loves the work. And she credits it all to the education she received from her joint degree program in law school:

> It came from my classroom experience at the school of education and working with Steve Taylor and getting an understanding of oppression and discrimination, something that I never, ever understood before. Ever. So I think actually, it could have happened to me in any area, I think, but it just happened to be disability rights and now that carries over to all these other areas of oppressed people.

C. FINDING PUBLIC INTEREST LAW EDUCATION IN LAW SCHOOL

Remember Erin McCormack from Chapter 3 who spends her summer vacations at a summer camp for children who are deaf? Knowing she would pursue public interest law from the start, she sought out a law school with a public-interest-friendly curriculum. As Crystal Doody's story exhibits, there are also gems of public interest legal education that shine through a law school's curriculum even though the law school is not known for its public interest law emphasis. Erin McCormack had heard and read of NYU School of Law's emphasis on public interest law, and she made sure it permeated the entire curriculum. There are several law schools that maintain well-deserved reputations for their comprehensive support of public interest law, NYU among the leaders. The importance of public interest law to the educational goals, philosophy, and curriculum of City University of New York (CUNY) Law School is a close rival to NYU. A woman attorney I interviewed, who wishes to stay anonymous, chose CUNY for that reason.

Sandy (pseudonym)

Sandy knows exactly where her passion for helping others comes from. Her grandmother was a social worker. Her dad, now retired, was a public school teacher and her mother was an aide in the public school system. Her parents deliberately chose service to others above financial success and Sandy has embraced that value system. One reason for her choice is that "We might not have had fancy vacations but we spent a lot of time together, and it was good." Sandy grew up in Healdsburg, California, in the middle of Sonoma wine country, before it was discovered as a destination. In fact, Sandy mostly remembers plum orchards where the now famous grape vineyards grow.

Going to a small liberal arts undergraduate school in Stockton, California, the University of the Pacific, Sandy spent her summers during college doing volunteer work. She worked with kids in East Pasadena, teaching English and mathematics to children having trouble in school. Sandy also spent a summer during college in Portugal, helping to build a school. After graduating college, Sandy spent three and a half years working with homeless families in Los Angeles. She first volunteered with the Claretian Lay Missionaries and worked with Latin American refugees who were homeless in East Los Angeles. After that, she took a permanent position with a homeless shelter. Observing firsthand the horrors of being homeless, Sandy decided to go to law school, specifically to be able to practice homelessness prevention, in the form of eviction defense.

Knowing she would be practicing law for poor people, Sandy chose CUNY for law school. In her words, "I went to CUNY for a couple of reasons. When I was researching public interest law schools it was one of the top choices. I also didn't want to come out with a lot of debt. I preferred to go to a public law school, if I could. I knew that the work I was going to be doing wasn't going to lend itself to paying off student loans."

Sandy graduated from CUNY in 1993. She surprised herself in law school by "expanding" her interests, as she puts it, and ending up with a concentration in health law. After graduation, unable to find a legal services job, Sandy worked as a temporary paralegal at a large law firm and took both the New York and California bar exams. Finally, a position opened in the Bronx Legal Aid office in August 1994.

Her first job at Legal Aid was in the housing unit, and Sandy got to practice the law she envisioned doing when she entered law school. For six years, her clients were mostly people who were facing homelessness. She then had a brief stint with Queens Legal Services while on a leave of absence from Legal Aid, where she worked in a general practice unit. Sandy returned to the Bronx Legal Aid office and practiced in the family law unit for about a year. Then a position in the health law unit opened up, which she decided to pursue, and she has been practicing health law since 2001. Since August 2005 she has been the supervising attorney of the health law unit in the Manhattan Legal Aid office.

As far as her financial life is concerned, Sandy graduated from CUNY law school with about $25,000 of educational debt. Her first Legal Aid job paid $32,000. Legal Aid is unionized, so the salary increments are predictable. As a supervising attorney Sandy now enjoys a comfortable salary of approximately $95,000. By playing, as she puts it, "financial games," Sandy was able to pay off her law school debt in about ten years:

> My monthly payments varied because I kind of played financial games with myself. You know, the interest-free checks you can get from credit cards? Credit card companies will send you these checks. They're usually good for like six months and you don't pay any interest. So I would pay large chunks, maybe $2,000 or $3,000 on the student loans and then pay it off at $500 a month to get the interest down. So, I actually paid it off, I think, in half the time that they were good for. I think they were 30-year payoffs and I paid it off in actually about ten years. I just kept paying more than you needed to pay so that the interest wouldn't pile up.

Sandy describes the first five years after graduating from law school as "definitely a struggle" financially. The commitment to her clients and the work she does sustained her throughout those lean years. With her family background as a foundation, Sandy would not describe the lifestyle trade-offs as a sacrifice. She's chosen apartments with low rents in less expensive areas of New York City and the boroughs. She's always had roommates, either friends or partners, from law school on. During her early years, Sandy was always mindful of living frugally; for example, not taking expensive vacations, not having a car, and limiting choices on apartments. With this approach she was able to afford to purchase an apartment in Manhattan, but she sometimes still thinks twice about ordering more than one glass of wine when dining out. "You might not have two because you know you don't want the bill to be going up!" But, for Sandy, "it's not a different lifestyle than how I was raised so I don't think about it that much in terms of trade-offs." Helping her maintain that perspective is the work that she loves. For Sandy, it's an easy choice:

> Our clients are facing so many obstacles in their lives that if we can provide some buffer to that, it's really great. Our practice is all about health care. We have clients who need surgeries and they can't get them. We have the opportunity to do something to assist someone in getting medically necessary care. It's . . . fabulous.

Sandy also enjoys the policy work she gets a chance to accomplish. In the 2006 state legislative session, severe Medicaid cuts were proposed. Working with a broad coalition of advocates across New York State, Sandy was one of a few lawyers responsible for making sure most of the cuts didn't happen and her clients would still have access to the health care they need.

At the forefront of her mind when Sandy ponders what advice she has for law students pursuing public interest law is the competition for the jobs available. She stresses the importance of having a track record in public interest work during law school, even if it means volunteering. The public interest jobs in major metropolitan areas are the most competitive and so Sandy would encourage truly dedicated folks to look outside the cities. Sandy observes that, "I have some friends who are in rural areas. Those offices often have a harder time filling positions. But, the lifestyle can be incredible. Sometimes the trade-off is that the pay is less but you might be able to manage debt easier in a less expensive location." Whatever it takes to pursue the dream, the reward is the satisfaction that comes from the work.

D. THE COST OF LEGAL EDUCATION

Law students originally on the path of becoming public interest lawyers are discouraged in that quest not only by the prevalent neglect of public interest law in the curriculum, but also by the incredibly high cost of legal education.[32] As educational debt mounts to $100,000 or more,[33] only the truly committed do not feel a tug toward the perceived and actual higher salaries of law firms and the private sector. The faint-hearted begin a free fall toward higher paying private sector and corporate jobs and away from the public interest law pursuits of their early law school ambitions.

State LRAPs, law school LRAPs, and LRAPs in certain legal services offices help alleviate the debt burden.[34] The recently enacted federal loan forgiveness program has the potential to significantly reduce the loan payments faced by public interest lawyers (although we saw in at least one representative case, Crystal Doody,

---

32. In 2006, law school tuition ranged from $14,245 a year at a state school for a resident student to $21,905 for a nonresident student to $30,520 a year at a private school. The average amount borrowed by law students over the course of the three years of law school was $54,509 for a state school and $83,181 for a private school. http//:www.abanet.org/legaled/statistics/charts/stats%20.

33. Including educational debt from undergraduate school.

34. Please see Appendix A for a complete list of loan repayment assistance programs.

her loan payments will actually be higher for the initial ten years of the federal program). The high cost of legal education and the low wages of public interest law jobs serve to deter all but the truly courageous and dedicated from pursuing public interest law careers. Even those brave hearts intent on finding happiness in public interest law despite finding little support or camaraderie in law school are often derailed by the cost of legal education, the high debt burden, and the low wages of public interest jobs. Michael Mulé and Michelle W. are two public interest lawyers who remain on track despite enormous debt loads.

Michael remains steadfast in his commitment to public interest law. His specialty is representing people with language barriers to fairness in obtaining their legal rights. One such person was a Spanish-speaking man who was fired from his job and denied unemployment benefits. There was a dispute about the incident that led up to the client's firing and Michael represented him in the appeal of the denial of his unemployment benefits. Michael works at a public interest law office in Rochester, New York. The hearings on appeal are heard in Buffalo, New York, about 60 miles away. When Michael received the notice of the hearing on the appeal, it stated that the client would be provided a telephone conference due to the fact that the client was a Spanish speaker. Michael ended up driving the client to Buffalo for the hearing because he determined that the judge would have to see the client in person to assess his credibility and believe his side of the story as to what led to his unfair dismissal. Finding in favor of Michael's client, the judge noted in her opinion that part of what swayed her was the client's demeanor at the hearing and she noted the value of the in-person appearance. Knowing that this opportunity would benefit all Spanish-speaking people going before the Appeals Board, Michael researched the issue and found out that as far back as 1983 the Appeals Board had been sued over the lack of interpreters and had agreed to provide interpreters to Spanish-speaking claimants. Michael contacted the judge, who immediately took it up with the Chief Judge of the Appeals Board. A week later the Chief Judge notified Michael that all Spanish-speaking claimants in Rochester would be afforded an in-person hearing in Rochester with an interpreter.

Michael Mulé

Hanna Cohn was a much-beloved public interest attorney who, at the time of her death, directed the Volunteer Legal Services Project, a program that provides free legal help to low-income residents of Monroe County, New York. When she died suddenly in the prime of her life, her family established a foundation and a two-year fellowship program in her honor at the Empire Justice Center in Rochester, New York. Michael Mulé is the second recipient of the two-year fellowship, having received the position after graduating from law school in May 2005. The project Michael works on during this two-year fellowship is representing people who face legal obstacles due to limited proficiency in the English language. Michael also works on disability rights and civil rights cases at the Empire Justice Center. Another one of Michael's cases involves a woman who is deaf and needs an interpreter to assist in communication. After going to a hospital emergency room for help with emotional issues, she was admitted to a 21-day program at the hospital, with arrangements made for her to temporarily reside at a facility operated by a government agency. The woman requested an interpreter at the residence but did not receive one at any time during her three-week stay there, nor did they provide TTY service so she could use the telephone or a computer so she could have e-mail access to her family. Michael has sued the facility in federal district court.

Michael graduated from Union Law School in Albany, New York, almost $115,000 in debt, $20,000 of that being from undergraduate school at the State University of New York at Albany. Motivated to attend law school after studying abroad in Italy for a semester in college and becoming interested in international policy and legal issues, Michael saw law school as an avenue to pursue his interest in international law, especially international human rights, international disability rights, and comparative law and policy issues. He accomplished a comparative study of the United Kingdom discrimination laws and participated in the Civil Rights and Disability Law Clinic in law school. He worked for the State Attorney General's office, in its consumer protection bureau, for a summer and another summer he spent interning at the Empire Justice Center office in Albany. A fluent Spanish speaker, Michael appreciates his fellowship at the Empire Justice Center because it affords him the ability to really learn the civil rights law and justice system in the United States to give him a basis of comparison with systems in other countries.

The educational debt Michael accumulated is primarily from the $26,000 annual tuition at Union Law School and his living expenses. After needing to take the first semester of law school over due to academic difficulties, Michael achieved honors and received several scholarships in law school. The debt he's facing would be higher but for those scholarships and the LRAP from his law school. His first year out of law school, practicing public interest law, Michael was eligible for and received a $3,700 check from Union Law School, which he used to pay down his private loan with the highest interest. The LRAP has a $10,000 cap, so he will only be eligible for it for two more years. Paying off a big chunk of the private loan gave Michael a three-year reprieve from payments so his monthly loan payments are $400 a month. Michael explains:

> The reason my payments are so low each month is because I really like to research and I really looked into rates and I figured out that if you consolidate with an American Bar Association membership at the consolidation place I went to you get a 1 percent interest rate discount. It's through the Access Loan Group. If you make 48 consecutive payments you get another ¼ percent knocked off. So, I could be at 3 percent in a couple of years.

With an annual salary of $35,000, Michael's diligence in searching out the best consolidation plan was essential. Doing work he enjoys, is interested in, and feels good about is much more important to Michael than the money he earns. He reflects, "I can't let the money determine what I'm interested in. I feel it would be a real sacrifice to say I need to go where the money is to be out of this debt and sacrifice being able to enjoy what I do every day and actually feel interested in what I'm doing." Michael compares the educational loan payments he's facing over the next 30 years to people who have mortgage payments to deal with, accepting that he's paying to have a job he loves rather than a house. Having just graduated from college, Michael is used to the "just barely above bare bones" lifestyle his salary demands and credits his value system with the choices he's made to do the work he does. "I don't really know what that's from but it's always just been there. I don't really see how I can value all the opportunities I've had if I can't help others with those skills. I think we're given certain opportunities for reasons and we should appreciate it even if we don't understand the reasons," Michael says.

Michael could talk all day about the cases he handled in the five months after he graduated from law school. He shared his work experiences with an extremely high level of excitement and enthusiasm. One of the major advantages of being at a public interest law office is that he's had his own clients since day two and has already filed his first federal civil rights case which will impact hundreds of people who are disabled. His client, who is deaf, was denied access to any means of communication via TTY for 21 days at a state-run health facility. Knowing that the client would not have been able to get a private attorney to take her case, Michael is grateful that he's in a position to assist her. "She doesn't care about the money. She cares about her friends. If they need those services someday she knows she did something to help them get those services."

Michael is also concerned about the bigger picture and wants to impact the system so that more law students will feel able to pursue public interest law. He thinks law schools need to do a much better job at working with law students to understand the debt they're getting into from their first year. Law schools receive their tuition payments from those loans and should be more proactive in helping law students with financial planning and debt counseling. The lack of assistance in this regard impacts students wishing to pursue careers in public interest law much more severely than their colleagues pursuing higher paying jobs in private practice. During law school, students are overwhelmed with their educational responsibilities, studying, and integrating new knowledge into their understanding of the law and its applications. Most law students know they're going to have a lot of debt but have no concept of how much debt they'll be in when they graduate, or how that debt will affect their career choices. Michael encourages law schools to do more to prepare law students for the debt they will have to manage. He remembers how it hit him during the final days of law school:

> I think the financial planning aspect is really one of the biggest downfalls of any law school. They're not concerned. They're concerned that they're going to get paid; I understand that. But they're not concerned with how you're going to pay once you get out. I think that's a real failure. It's called the exit interview with the financial aid office. It's pretty much just a stack of all the different loans that were processed for you throughout your three years. They tell you, "Here's some places you can call to consolidate. Good luck." It was a half-hour meeting. It was a group of us; it wasn't even individual. You got your stack and you say okay I guess I owe $115,000 now, out of the blue. But there was not time for that because you started bar review the following week.

In addition to law schools working harder with students on financial planning, especially those students interested in public interest law, Michael hopes that more public interest law and legal services offices will develop LRAPs. This incredibly energetic 26-year-old is putting his exhaustive research abilities to use in assessing such programs throughout the country to help his office create an LRAP. Michael hopes that his office will create a sustainable model for legal services offices throughout the state that will be financially viable for the offices and an incentive to continue to attract the best and brightest attorneys to public interest work. Michael's enthusiasm, altruism, and passion are infectious.

Michelle W.

Michelle W. has always "felt it a spiritual calling to serve the poor." After growing up Catholic, Michelle now disavows the Catholic Church due to their treatment of gays and lesbians, their stance on women's issues, and the recent sex abuse scandals. Michelle is quick to point out, though, that:

> I firmly believe in the gospel principles that I learned and believed as a Catholic and that I continue to believe. I decided that my life should be about Jesus' message and the gospel principles about serving the poor and the needy and the underrepresented. We have so much wealth and so much power in this country and yet we have homeless people and people who are hungry and people who have no health care and I just find that abhorrent. So, applying those religious, gospel values to the real world just seemed like what I should do with my life. So that's why I do this.

What Michelle has been doing since 2001 is working at Legal Assistance Foundation of Metropolitan Chicago as a staff attorney in the HIV/AIDS Project. In 1989, when Michelle was in her mid-20s, she became personally involved in the care of a friend who was HIV positive. That experience inspired her to first volunteer with an AIDS hospice, working with people who were dying. When she moved to western Michigan a few years later and was told there was no agency through which she could volunteer to work with people living with AIDS, she decided to create one. The organization she founded helped people diagnosed with HIV or AIDS with basic needs such as food and transportation and also created a buddy program.

A community education component followed. It was through that work that Michelle decided to go to law school:

> While doing that work I was trying to connect people with AIDS to social security benefits and getting public aid. Certainly, lots of people were being discriminated against in all kinds of areas. Instead of being on the periphery of that, and referring clients to other sources, I wanted to be someone who could do something about those discrimination issues and that's when I decided to go to law school specifically to do AIDS law.

Michelle entered law school in 1999 in her mid-30s knowing exactly what type of public interest law she wanted to practice and why. She chose DePaul University College of Law in Chicago because it was one of only a handful of law schools throughout the country that had an AIDS law curriculum and an active gay and lesbian law student organization. It also helped that DePaul was founded on the principles of St. Vincent dePaul who, as a priest in France, "organized wealthy, socialite women to serve soup to the poor in Paris," in Michelle's words. "That's exactly what I wanted to do and I found that the Vincentian mission of serving the poor fit exactly with why I was going to law school." The one deficiency — that DePaul Law School did not have an LRAP — did not worry Michelle too much because people in both the Admissions Office and the Dean's Office told her that they were looking into creating an LRAP and Michelle had reason to believe that the LRAP would be created during the three years she was attending law school or soon thereafter. Unfortunately, the dean at the time, who was very supportive of an LRAP and worked hard with Michelle and other students to create it, died tragically soon after Michelle graduated from law school. The process of getting an LRAP was delayed and, although DePaul did get an LRAP in 2005, it was too late for Michelle. That would have a huge impact on Michelle's finances and her ability to pay back her student loans. Michelle sadly admits:

> I racked up a ton of debt on tuition and supporting myself during law school and I hoped that something good would happen and I would be able to make ends meet, but my loans went into default. Not because I was shirking my responsibility to pay on my loans but because I couldn't make the level of payments the lenders wanted. I thought I could make payments based on my income level, but that was only granted for a short time. Then they wanted more than I could pay.

Because the tuition at DePaul was close to $20,000 a semester when Michelle attended, and she didn't have any grants, scholarships, or substantial outside income, Michelle graduated with about $120,000 in debt. Michelle did work at the Legal Assistance Foundation during her second and third years of law school but, as a law clerk, the pay was very little. The debt she incurred in law school included some for living expenses.

For the first two years after law school, Michelle worked at Prairie State Legal Services in Waukegan, Illinois. She returned to the Legal Assistance Foundation (LAF) in 2001 when a position opened in the HIV Project. When she returned to LAF she was earning approximately $39,000 a year. She was able to receive a deferral on some of the loan payments and then, based on an income-sensitive payment plan that she thought was long-term, she was paying about $600 a month on her school loans. When the payments increased to $1,000 a month she defaulted and the loan company sued her and she is now having her wages garnished. Michelle says, "The ironic thing is that in trying to settle the case when it went to court I offered to pay them more than what they're getting in the garnishment because it's a statutory 15 percent cap that they can take. I was willing to stretch and pay them a little more than that but I guess they wanted the judgment so payment would be guaranteed through a garnishment order." Now earning close to $50,000 a year,

Michelle's economic difficulties have not eased much and she maintains a very modest lifestyle. She reflects:

> I don't own a car. I don't own property. I live a pretty modest lifestyle. I buy all my clothes at outlet stores or second-hand shops. I'm not complaining about that, I don't mind living a modest lifestyle. I was perfectly willing to do that; that was my part of the sacrifice of doing this kind of law. But, I certainly think that our government and our society and my law school could chip in as well, because we're doing the work of the people. We're taking care of our people and our society. I think it should be valued more, and I think society would value it more if they knew the kind of financial sacrifice it is to pay for law school and then do public interest work. I think part of it is the bad reputation that attorneys, that attorneys are self-serving and just out to make a lot of money and I don't think people really think about what public interest lawyers do or that we're so low paid. Our society needs to put more resources behind public interest work because really dedicated people just can't afford to do this kind of work with the skyrocketing cost of law school.

It was obviously very hard for Michelle to discuss her financial difficulties, the wage garnishment, and the consequences of decisions she feels she might be harshly judged about. To speak of these sensitive subjects knowing they would be published and become public was very difficult for her, even knowing her identity could be anonymous. The importance of bringing a voice to poor people in need of lawyers who can maintain the financial ability to work in the public interest is what motivates Michelle to continue:

> Part of it is my real commitment to working with people with AIDS. It's a passion of mine and there aren't enough of us doing this kind of work. I don't

mind if I don't own property. That is probably a big difference. I also figure that some people need to stick it out and do this work — somebody has to keep doing this work, why not me? So I guess that's sort of the "calling" aspect of it. I don't mean to sound like some kind of martyr or anything. I don't mean that at all. I just feel dedicated to it.

Knowing how hard it can be financially, Michelle would advise law students to plan ahead even when deciding which law school to attend. Think about going to a state school or work for a couple of years between college and law school to save money. Be relentless in your quest for grants and scholarships to help pay tuition. Look for the law schools that have established LRAP programs. And, above all, "Don't give up hope. If you feel dedicated to this kind of work, in my opinion, it's worth the sacrifice."

When asked if there was anything else she wanted to add, Michelle didn't hesitate to say:

There is one other comment. My clients live on $603 a month on social security benefits. If they can do that I can live on my salary and I feel rich compared to them. It's hard for me to complain about living modestly when they can barely live at all. It's hard for me to complain about my circumstances when my clients are in front of me every day with much greater struggles.

If legal services attorneys weren't here to help protect the poorest of the poor's rights they'd be completely trampled. There would be no one to protect their rights. I don't mean to sound cheesy but that's what our country is founded on, that everyone gets these rights. That's the basis of our justice system. For example, there was a study done on pro-se litigants in the Chicago eviction court. Their bench trials lasted 90 seconds if they were not represented and they were summarily evicted and generally given seven days to move and they're effectively homeless. If we're not there their rights just don't get protected and represented. I think it's critical that we not only support legal services, but also expand legal services. Our current legal services system doesn't have enough resources to represent everyone who needs representation. We've got to keep doing this work and it's got to be better funded.

E. CUTTING COSTS

As did "Sandy," who went to the City University of New York law school due to its public-interest-law-friendly curriculum and its comparably low tuition, some law students intent on pursuing public interest law seek out state law schools for their low tuition Many private law schools maintain generous scholarship funds and financial aid packages that can be accessed but, if they're not available, state schools are an option. Angie and Kathy, who chose to remain anonymous, knew they would be entering the field of public interest law, anticipated low salaries, and spent their three years of law school at state schools.

Angie (pseudonym)

The first thing one notices about Angie is her intensity. Angie's dedication to and seriousness about the work she does is written on her face. She has been working in the area of domestic violence for many years, both before and after obtaining her Juris Doctor; her commitment to this extremely intense area of practice has never wavered. Angie confides, "I think to stay in this field is definitely a calling. I don't think it's for everyone. And I do feel a call to the work." In reflecting on her nearly two decades working in the domestic violence arena Angie says:

> I think that it's a field that I've seen change and evolve significantly since I started working in the field in the

late '80s. There's no comparison between the amount of federal and state funding and the attention that's gone into that field. It was very exciting to be a part of a movement that was exploding around you over the last 20 years. It's pretty amazing all the changes that have taken place. There's a greater awareness. It's been fun to be a part of that ride for the field, good and bad. That was very interesting to me.

The ride started for Angie after attaining her bachelor's degree from Drew University in New Jersey. Her first job out of college was counseling adult and child victims of domestic violence at a domestic violence shelter where she was earning poverty-level wages. Admitting now that it was a "pretty high burnout field," she also worked with runaway and homeless youth in a youth program for about two-and-a-half years before deciding to attend law school. In her domestic violence work, Angie had been a court advocate and she recalls that "Once I got into the law field it was very clear to me that doing work as an attorney was where I wanted to be." She adds, "Also, just seeing from an advocacy point of view as a court advocate and not as a lawyer, seeing what I perceive to be a lot of injustices at that time, pretty blatant injustices, it was very compelling for me to enter the field and stay in the field."

Knowing she would pursue a public interest law career, Angie chose a state school, the State University of New York at Buffalo, for law school. The low tuition was a definite draw, as was the fact that it had a family violence clinic. To further her ability to be self-supporting when she graduated, Angie worked in a private firm her second and third years of law school. Her third year she had two jobs, as she also worked as a research assistant for a professor, and she had a full-time course load. She paid for her first year with money from her grandmother; Angie had to take out loans to pay for her second and third years of law school. She graduated $39,000 in debt. After the grace period, about nine months after graduation, Angie's monthly payments on her loans were approximately $650. It took two months for Angie to realize that she wasn't going to be able to pay bills and keep up the loan payments. At the time, she was working her first job out of law school with the Legal Aid Society of Rochester in the domestic violence legal unit. The job she had gone to law school for was hers, representing victims of domestic violence exclusively on family law matters such as divorce, child support, custody, visitation, and orders of protection. Earning less than $30,000 a year, Angie had to restructure her loan term from ten to 20 years but her payments went down to a manageable $300 a month.

Due to the high burnout rate among those in domestic violence work, evident among attorneys as well as advocates, Angie always had the long-term goal of doing policy work in the field. She was provided that opportunity with the job she has held since March 2002 at the Empire Justice Center in Rochester. As the state support person for legal services attorneys involved in direct representation of domestic violence cases, Angie provides technical assistance, research support, and training to legal services attorneys throughout the state. A grant from the State Coalition Against Domestic Violence funds Angie in providing technical assistance and legal support to domestic violence shelters throughout the state. In her words:

> When I started here I think I was on my way to getting pretty burned out. I had clients who died or took their own lives or things like that. It's very hard work at that level all the time. I just found a way to do the work. I always intended to do policy-oriented work; I just didn't necessarily intend to do it 2½ years out of law school. The timing was right for me to do this. It's a great way to work in the field without having to actually do the work that really creates enormous burnout and to support the people who are challenged by the work that they're doing every day.

When Angie started the job at the Empire Justice Center she was earning $32,000 a year. She now earns $45,000. With a domestic partner who's in the early years of a second career as an architect, their joint finances barely enabled them to buy a home. Angie had lived in an apartment much longer than she wanted to and had driven an old car for a long time. As she describes, "I ended up being self-indulgent and buying a new car in 2002 when my old one kept breaking down." The car she bought was "a low-end Mazda." She and her partner tried to finance their home purchase with both a mortgage and a home equity loan but Angie couldn't qualify as the primary borrower on the home equity loan because, with her student loan payments and her car payment, her debt-to-income ratio was too high. Angie's architect partner could have qualified but the interest rate that she qualified for was too high to make the deal acceptable. They ended up buying the house through a straight, 30-year mortgage. The financial stretch of buying a house has not left much flexibility in their financial lives. What's weighing on Angie's mind and budget most heavily now is their desire to have children and their inability to afford day care or for Angie to work part time to raise the children. As Angie says:

> Those are the things I don't think I thought I would have to compromise on like children or planning for children. I knew that I wouldn't necessarily be someone who would go to France every year or to Hawaii and I'm okay with that. Those are the compromises that I don't mind. Those aren't really important to me. But things like having a kid or a home, I don't think I anticipated compromises on that stuff.

She offers the following advice for others on the same path: "Do your best to structure your life. Really determine what your priorities are and then think about it. I work in a public interest firm that's more family friendly but, if I can't take advantage of having a family then those policies don't do anything for me. Really evaluate what your priorities are and be willing to make sacrifices." Angie is willing to make those sacrifices except perhaps when it's time to finally make the decision about children. They're waiting to see how the finances work out after they're in the house awhile but, at the age of 39, Angie doesn't feel she can give herself too much more time to decide. The choice will be extremely hard for her. As she ponders the options, she says, "It never really occurred to me to do anything different. It just never occurred to me to do anything but public-service-oriented work."[35]

Kathy (pseudonym)

Kathy grew up in a family where fairness and a sense of justice were instilled at an early age. Her parents have core values that include a high priority on treating all people fairly. Kathy reflects that her father would "speak the same to the governor of the state as he would to the Vietnamese family my parents helped when they first came over." Neither of her parents sees class distinctions. They treat all people with respect and fairness because "it's the right thing to do." Kathy credits her parents with her interest in justice and fairness issues, which led to her becoming a public interest lawyer. She also credits her parents with her lack of focus on money. "My parents are very good people, and they never had a focus on money. It was never important for them to have a new car. It was important for them to be able to provide for their kids and send us to school. We both [she and her brother] went to undergrad without debt and we both went to Catholic high schools which were not terribly expensive. That was important to them. They've never been focused on having a nice house and they've never been into material things."

Kathy's brother also does public interest work for a homelessness coalition in Colorado. Instilled with their parents' values, they both entered the Peace Corps after college. Having a sense of humor has always kept the family in good stead. Not placing a high priority on money, her father has worked for the state of New York and her mom has always worked in the home and volunteered for many nonprofit organizations. Kathy describes her mom as "incredibly

---

35. As an update, Angie reports that after the first year of home ownership, she and her partner feel financially secure enough to decide to start a family (phone call with Angie, Oct. 23, 2007).

generous," volunteering for an after-school program for inner-city kids and helping recently immigrated Vietnamese families.

Growing up in this family led Kathy to know at an early age that she would spend her working years helping people in some way. She decided in college that she would go to law school for public interest law, mostly by process of elimination. "If I was smart enough to become a doctor, I would have become a doctor. If I had patience, I would have become a teacher. But, in terms of useful professions to help the world, I didn't have those skills. But, I do argue well, so I went to law school." She considers herself very fortunate to have known exactly what she wanted to do in life and to have discovered how she would do it.

Although she knew that she'd attend law school, Kathy spent almost five years working between graduation from a small liberal arts college in Massachusetts in 1989 and the start of law school. Part of the time she traveled; for a year she worked as an administrative assistant at a not-for-profit foundation in Chicago, and had her first exposure to disability law. The bulk of the time was spent in the Peace Corps. She speaks glowingly of her time in Thailand, where she taught English and provided AIDS education. The town she was assigned to by the Peace Corps was about eight hours northwest of Bangkok, a very rural village with about 2,000 people, 20 minutes from the nearest grocery store. She loved it.

Having been out of college for five years, one of the reasons Kathy chose Temple University for law school was because it has a higher median age for entering students. Most of the friends she made in law school had taken time off between undergraduate education and law school. One of her closest friends celebrated her 50th birthday while at Temple. Kathy loved law school, loved the classes, and loved the fact that the professors at Temple were so accessible. She knows her time working and in the Peace Corps after college led her to appreciate law school and led her to take advantage of the educational opportunities much more than she had in college.

Another paramount concern for Kathy in choosing which law school to attend was cost. She remembers panicking at one point, thinking "What if I get out and I'm not able to afford to go into public interest law? That would be defeating the whole purpose for going to law school." At Temple, students are eligible for in-state tuition after their first year, and that was a huge factor for Kathy, determined to keep costs and her subsequent debt to a minimum. A final consideration in choice of law school was that Temple was in a big city (Philadelphia) and, although she loved the people and the little village in Thailand, she was really ready to be in a big city.

When she graduated from law school, Kathy had $70,000 in educational debt. At first, her monthly payments were over $1,000. She definitely notices the irony in the fact that her work involves advising people about their finances, yet she admits being a terrible money manager herself. It was really hard meeting the monthly payments her first year out with a salary of only about $30,000 a year. If not for some money her grandmother left her that she used to pay the student loans, Kathy would have been in serious trouble. The trouble caught up with her, though, in the third or fourth year of paying the loans, when she defaulted. Once there's a default on private student loans, the lender is able to go straight to collection and the lender contacted Kathy's employer, which totally rattled her. Remembering that time, Kathy reflects, "When you can't pay your loans, yeah, it's awful stress . . . awful, awful stress . . . awful stress." She knew if they garnished her wages she wouldn't be able to live so she took the unprecedented step of allowing her father to pay off a significant amount of her loans and she consolidated the rest. For a long time after that, her monthly payments were up to $600, but now that she has two of the loans paid off, she pays almost $300 a month. Kathy credits the time of defaulting on her loans with making her a better advocate for her clients. Laughing, she says, "I get the not answering phone calls because of debt. I get that it's very real."

The lawyering work Kathy does now is in the consumer law area. She works for a statewide legal services office mostly representing low-income folks about to lose their homes through predatory mortgage lending scams. Kathy also works on fair debt collection issues and fair credit reporting problems. Graduating from Temple University in 1997, she worked for a year in a public interest law center in Philadelphia, providing representation in disability law matters and some housing discrimination cases. She then worked for five years with Community Legal Services in Philadelphia, where she began her consumer law practice, and transferred those skills to her current job in 2003. Despite the stress of debt over the years and knowing that her commitment to public interest law means resigning herself to never having a lot of money, Kathy has no regrets. She says, "I totally love my job. I love what I do." And, if she dies tomorrow, she wants to know she was doing meaningful work up to the last moment.

There are serious trade-offs she's making in life to do the work she loves. As a single woman, the knowledge that she can't afford a child on her salary prevents Kathy from pursuing that dream. At a time when she's seeing friends buy their second homes, Kathy wonders if her car will make it for the short commute home. Kathy reflects, "I think the stress is a big thing. I'm not interested in material things. I don't need a new car. I don't need a big house. I don't need a lot of stuff at home. I don't really care about clothes. I mean, I'm happy with that trade-off, happy to deal with that trade-off. I've always looked at my job as a really expensive car. A luxury car, right? People have Jaguars, I have a job that I love."

Kathy was able to buy a small, one-bedroom house. With her monthly housing costs of over $1,000 and a salary of $49,000 a year in Albany, New York, Kathy feels she's always just about making it financially. "Whenever I get a little bit of money it always has to be spent somewhere. It's a very stressful way to live. I hate it. Hate it when I think about it. And the alternative is what? To go work for a firm, and not do what I went to law school for? Just not going to do that." Although she does not take expensive vacations, Kathy finds a way every couple of years to travel, albeit third class and staying in hostels. She also confesses to buying a ski pass every year. Still, she knows that people who can survive financially in legal services jobs generally have some backup resources. As hard as it was, she's allowed her parents to bail her out at times. "I used to joke that I would always take out payday loans from my parents. I'm no different than my clients except that my parents don't charge a

265 percent interest rate for a payday loan." Kathy expresses the sense that most legal services lawyers who stay in legal services a long time have a "backer"; a significant other, spouse, or parent helping them out.

If legal services programs don't take action to create LRAPs, in Kathy's opinion, only lawyers with independent resources or coming from or marrying into privilege will be able to sustain themselves financially. The trade-off for the public interest law profession in general will be a much less diverse community of lawyers. With that in mind, she's been a strong advocate for an LRAP at her office and advises anyone interested in public interest work thinking of going to law school to choose their law school based on the LRAP. Law students just don't have a sense of how onerous student loans can be, as most never had a monthly payment to think about in their lives. As someone deeply committed to public interest law, who loves her job and can't imagine doing any other kind of work, Kathy also knows the stress of the financial trade-offs she's making to pursue the work she loves. She personifies being passionate about public interest work. Just as strongly, she personifies being passionate about institutional support of the lawyers willing to make the trade-offs.

F. PASSION VERSUS THE PAYCHECK: LOVING THE WORK AND LIVING WITH THE WAGES

Public interest law jobs are admittedly low-paying, as law jobs go. Money cannot be your primary motivator if you're going to sustain a passion for the work while making the financial trade-offs. Luckily, job satisfaction has not been correlated with the size of one's paycheck and the lawyers in this book bear out the results of the studies that have been conducted on this phenomenon. We've already witnessed some of the ways public interest lawyers manage, both fiscally and psychically, with their public interest wages. Jonathan Feldman and Esperanza Colón provide two more examples of how to finesse the trade-offs. Jonathan and his family moved from the

New York City area to upstate New York to realize their dream of home ownership. Esperanza Colón makes conscious choices every day to support herself and her daughter on her paycheck from Legal Aid. As is the case with all the other lawyers we've met so far, Jonathan and Esperanza could not imagine doing anything else with their law degrees other than the public interest work they love.

Jonathan Feldman

Jonathan Feldman graduated from NYU Law School in 1988, before their famous LRAP was born. The reputation of NYU as a law school that was highly supportive of public interest law was, however, fully entrenched. Jonathan chose NYU law over the other schools he was accepted into because of its public interest law reputation. The ethos of Jonathan's family and the experiences he availed himself of in high school and college led him to seek out a legal education centered around creating a just society. During college he sought out summer internships working on housing and homelessness issues in the Washington, DC area where he grew up. Jonathan remembers, "In one of my internships I came across some of the materials from New York City cases where the lawyers were trying to argue for the right for housing for the homeless under the New York State constitution, so that's actually what got me thinking about going to law school. That was in 1983 and then I went to law school in 1985. That was my goal."

He found that and more at NYU. He found a community of students dedicated to public interest work and a faculty and administration who validated the importance of that work. He also found the *Journal of Law and Social Change* and, as an editor surrounded by others with a similar passion for social justice, had a fun and rewarding experience.

With some financial support in law school, Jonathan graduated in 1988 with $20,000 in school loans. As Jonathan says, "It was manageable but not negligible, especially with my salary when I got out." His grandmother contributed partially to his tuition for one year and, for several reasons, not the least being financial,

Jonathan worked at one of the big private law firms in New York City the summer after his second year in law school, which he describes as "an interesting contrast." He made almost $15,000 in one summer, which significantly helped defray costs for his third year of law school. Reflecting that "I could have come out with more debt but it was still enough to make an impact," Jonathan has been paying back his school loans now for almost 20 years.

After graduating law school, Jonathan clerked for a federal district judge in Philadelphia for two years. His starting salary was $27,000 a year. Then in 1990, he started work at the Education Law Center in Newark, New Jersey, a small public interest organization. The many opportunities to work on high-impact class action litigation cases, which Jonathan would have over the years, began there. A major school financing case, challenging the equities of public school financing, had been ongoing for 20 years. As Jonathan started work at the Education Law Center, the case came to a critical juncture. Jonathan explains, "It was a great time to be there. There was a trial on whether the legislature had complied with the court directive, and so I got to cross-examine expert witnesses and put on witnesses at the trial and do all these tons of appellate briefs. It was great. Just two years out of a clerkship to work on a case like that was really fortuitous." Similarly, when he changed jobs in 1993 and started lawyering at the Community Service Society in New York City, a major civil rights class action was gearing up. The Community Service Society is a large welfare rights organization. As he started work there in 1993, the Motor Voter Law had just been passed by Congress, and Jonathan worked on the challenges to states that didn't comply. "We would sue them and force them to comply. I got to play a really cool role in all that litigation from 1993 to 1997. We won virtually all the cases."

By the time the voting rights cases were winding down, Jonathan and his wife had their first child and were feeling the pinch of his public interest law salary, which in 1997 was in the low $50,000 range. He had maxed out on promotions, advancing from staff attorney to associate counsel at the Society. Jonathan's wife worked at the time as a contract archeologist, preparing archeological impact statements for construction projects. She loved the work but it was also low paying. Starting a family, living in an apartment in Maplewood, New Jersey, and commuting to work, they began to weigh their options in the home ownership department. Even within a large radius of New York City, encompassing central New Jersey, they could not afford their own home. Remembering the time, Jonathan recalls, "I actually interviewed at a few firms, sort of boutique firms in New York City and still, that wasn't what I wanted to do. Either we had to make more money or move if we wanted to buy a house." Although he really liked his job at Community Services Society and would have stayed if the salary was higher, Jonathan and his wife "started thinking about maybe we should move to a low-cost area. Where can we actually afford to continue to work in public interest?" That's when his current job, at the Empire Justice Center in Rochester, New York, appeared. A big motivation for the move, in addition to the attractiveness of the work he would be doing, was the low cost of housing in Rochester. "When I came here I took a seven or eight-thousand-dollar pay cut to the low $40s, but because housing was so much cheaper here we thought with our savings we could probably buy a house. And we did. We were able to buy a house here, but we probably couldn't have in most places in the country."

Making the move to upstate New York provided Jonathan the opportunity to continue to work on the cases he loves. At the Empire Justice Center he primarily handles education law cases and some other civil rights issues, and has been able to bring class action cases, litigating for expansive solutions to systemic civil rights violations. He's comfortable with the choices he's made and says, "I wanted to do this more than I wanted the money. I would like to be in a better financial position but that's not as important to me as being able to do the work that I'm doing." It reminds Jonathan of an economics professor he had at Oberlin, where he attended undergraduate college. This professor "always said you can't do good and also do well. I think he was right. It really is a trade-off." Whether one agrees with that sentiment or not, Jonathan has been consciously choosing doing good since he took his first job (after his two-year clerkship for the federal judge) with the Education Law Center. As mentioned, Jonathan had clerked the summer after his second year of law school at a private firm. He was offered an associate position at the firm when he graduated. The salary would have been $100,000 a year. Why didn't he take the offer? "They wined and dined us and it was fun for the summer but when we [the clerks] would leave to go play softball the associates were still there. I realized there was a whole different side to that law firm, to any law firm, plus it just wasn't what I was interested in. The issues they were working on just weren't the things that were exciting to me."

Since that time, Jonathan, his spouse, and their two beautiful children have continued to make the lifestyle choices needed to do good in the world. He's now earning about $63,000 a year. Jonathan's wife decided to change careers because there was too much travel involved in archaeological work to have enough time with her family. She went back to school for library science, graduated in 2004, and in the spring of 2006 started working about 20 hours a week as a reference librarian in the public library. Even though Jonathan's school loans are comparatively low, they had a succession of lean years financially while his wife was in school, years now paying off her school loans, and incurring day care expenses all along the way. He hopes, "Maybe in a few years once the three-year-old is older we'll be in a better position." These trade-offs are worth it in the balance. Jonathan is happy doing the work he does and knows that some of his buddies in the public interest programs at NYU are not as fortunate as he. In his words:

> Especially some people I know that wanted to do public interest work but didn't saying, "I'll do it later," but later never comes. They're partners in firms and I know a few of them are pretty unhappy from a personal standpoint. They definitely feel good about the money but I know some of them, ranging from actually feeling truly guilty about what they're doing because they never realized their dreams, what

they set out to do as well as just the work wearing down on them. In extreme cases I know a few people who didn't want to go down that path but did anyway and I think I'm certainly happier than they are. I hope that someday they might get the opportunity to do public interest work, because I know that they were as interested in it as I was.

Esperanza Colón

For people who haven't been there, thoughts of the South Bronx conjure up mostly stereotypical scenes of despair and hopelessness. At the end of the journey to the Legal Aid office, the reality is a thriving, vibrant, energetically complex neighborhood that dispels the stereotypical notions and images. Esperanza ("Espy") Colón grew up in the South Bronx, not very far from the Legal Aid office where she has worked since graduating from law school in 1992. She reflects the energy and vibrancy of the community. Espy loves the work she does, mostly practicing welfare law and disability law, with an occasional unemployment benefits case.

Esperanza (the meaning of her name, "Hope," should not be overlooked) remembers as a child watching the struggles of residents in her poor neighborhood who needed lawyers. She learned early on the importance of Legal Aid and access to strong and capable attorneys to maintain basic civil rights and subsistence needs. She received the offer to work at the South Bronx office the day she graduated from law school and remembers her incredible excitement and thinking, "Oh my God, I work at the Legal Aid Society. I used to hear about it all the time as a kid and I'm going to be an attorney there! What a nice gift! Thank you!"

There was no question in Espy's mind that she would go into public interest work. She chose Northeastern University Law School because of the co-op program it offered. The program provides law students with an opportunity to sample four different areas of law while they're in school, alternating 12 weeks of academic work with a 12-week cooperative internship, applying the legal theory learned to the actual practice of law. Espy used the co-op program to work for four different public interest employers in three different areas of the country.

Espy received a full scholarship at Northeastern University. Her $32,000 in debt when she graduated from law school accumulated due to living expenses as she worked hard to minimize her debt. She knows she's on the luckier end of the spectrum because many of her friends graduated with $100,000 of debt. Espy's comparatively small educational debt is partially a result of a very conscious effort to live simply, in addition to her tuition scholarship. She speaks of her frugality in a very matter-of-fact tone, accepting the sacrifices she's made to pursue the important goals and choices in her life. She took out loans for rent but lived in Newton, Massachusetts, where the cost of living was much less than Boston. School was a 45-minute commute every day on public transportation, but she deliberately rejected the idea of moving into Boston because of the endless temptations to spend money in the city. Living in the attic turned into living space of a house owned by the family who lived downstairs, she became friendly with them and was thankful for their generosity in sharing meals and letting her use their laundry facilities. Espy didn't take trips during her three years in law school except to a friend's family's house on Cape Cod. The one spring break trip Espy took in college, other than when her parents sent her money to travel home to the Bronx, was on a $98.00 American Express voucher to Boca Raton to stay at the house of a friend's parents. This trip was taken at a time most of her friends were traveling to places like Cancun for spring break. Espy doesn't characterize her lifestyle in terms of sacrifice because she views such expenditures as luxuries. Her "can-do" attitude and steadfast determination to pursue her dreams shine through as she relates cleaning houses on weekends and babysitting to earn money during law school. "I'd clean houses and actually made a lot of money that way and did a good job. I wasn't shy or ashamed or anything. I needed the money and that's pretty much how I got through law school."

When Espy started at Legal Aid in 1992, the starting salary was $29,000. She loved the job from the start, the client contact, the primary responsibility for case handling. Her first trial went all the way to the Appellate Division, and she was surprised and excited that she was able to do the case every step of the way (with as much guidance as she wanted), even arguing at the Appellate Division. The passion she felt for the work sustained her through difficult financial decisions.

Faced with initial loan payments of $750 a month, and unable to come up with a security deposit and money to move, she made the difficult decision to move back in with her parents. Although not her choice as an adult, the same resolute determination is evident as she reports, "It's just something I had to do." For two years her paycheck went mostly to her school loans until she consolidated her loans and the payments were reduced to a little under $300 a month. Then she was able to move out of her parents' home when she found a rent-stabilized apartment a friend was moving from. Espy's friend arranged with the landlady to keep the rent the same for Espy. Espy was fortunate in her next move because she was able to get her own apartment in a semisubsidized building outside of the high-cost city limits. Espy finally paid off her school loans after 14 years. The final two years she paid large amounts at once, applying tax refunds to loan payments, to get it paid as quickly as possible. By then, Espy had a two-year-old son and was paying nursery school tuition. A single mom, she is also keenly aware of the other perks of working at Legal Aid, including good medical benefits, generous vacation and personal time, as well as flexibility in scheduling the workday.

Espy's life is a lesson in living simply and within one's means. At a salary now close to six figures a year, she is able to do more than when she first graduated law school, but she knows it's a place where Legal Aid attorneys plateau in terms of salary (not to mention the cost of living in the New York metropolitan area). "I know that I will probably never make much more than I'm making now, but I'm okay with that. I really am okay with that." The trade-off for being able to do the work she loves to do is doing some of her shopping at 99-cent stores. She waxes poetic about the deals you can get, including greeting cards for two for a dollar and tissues for $1.50 less than most stores. Unashamed to clip coupons and going out to dinner rarely, Espy is a study in frugality. Oh, and she does not own a car.

What motivates Espy is that "I really, really enjoy what I'm doing." She has many friends in the private sector who hate their jobs, so she knows how fortunate she is to have a job she likes. "It's nice to see when someone comes in and they have a messy, messy case that you wind up fixing in the end and the person would not have been able to do that on their own and they're so grateful to you, and you just feel good." Espy sees so many clients struggling to make ends meet. She feels for working poor people who are trying to get out of the public assistance system but need a public assistance supplement that gets deducted from the amount they earn so they can never get out of the cycle of poverty. "A lot of people just make do, make do however they can and it's just a shame that people who are trying to get out of the system, the system is what's keeping them down rather than helping them get on their feet. So . . . my job is very rewarding. We're advocates for people who would not have the means to advocate for themselves and would just get lost in the red tape of all of these bureaucracies. Obviously, I'm not here because it's a noble thing to do. I really believe in this work."

G. FINDING THE GIFTS

Some pieces of advice and wisdom have a way of sticking with us and to us. It's a mystery as to why some wisdom sticks and some doesn't. For me, I'll never forget my senior year of college, still not knowing what I would do with this gift of life but knowing I wanted somehow to be in a helping profession. I was thinking about law school as a vehicle for my desire to have an impact on the lives of others but was extremely daunted by the cost of a legal education. I'll never forget the words of the head resident of the dorm where I lived. She was the wife of a professor. Tricia Gregory is her name. I doubt she knows what effect she had on my life. Her words were simple and to the point: "Don't let the money stop you." I had grown up in a lower middle-class family where my parents were always struggling with finances, an overpowering struggle at times. The lack of money had stopped me from many materialistic and nonmaterialistic desires and could have prevented my continued educational pursuits. My parents and I borrowed and worked so I could get through undergraduate school and, in the scarcity mindset, I could not see my way clear to think about law school past the problem of how I would pay for it because I knew my parents were tapped out. The simple words, "Don't let the money stop you," were words I had never heard before and would never have considered but for Tricia Gregory. Now I offer them to you, with more than 25 years of hindsight giving me the power and wisdom to know what great advice it is. Don't let the money stop you. Don't let the money stop you from one of the greatest careers and the most rewarding lives you can have.

Being on a journey guided by heart and soul and following one's passion does not take us down well-paved roads or paths indicated on the usual maps. Staying true to one's calling of becoming a public interest lawyer is full of challenges and obstacles, financial, emotional, and psychological. Public interest law remains at the fringes of legal education and the legal profession. Although we acknowledge that necessary legal assistance remains unattainable for most middle-income folks and almost all but a few fortunate low-income people, legal education and the legal profession cater mostly to law students and lawyers representing institutions, corporations, and high-income people. "The fact remains that fewer than one percent of our nation's lawyers provide legal services to the poor."[36] Law continues to perpetuate our societal power dynamic, maintaining rights for those who can afford expensive legal representation, and sacrificing the rights and lives of people who can't afford to hire attorneys. Justice for all remains an elusive ideal with a few aspiring lawyers pursuing the dream. If all law students who entered

---

36. David C. Vladeck, *supra* note 27 at 352. *See also* William P. Quigley, *supra* note 27; Patrick J. Schlitz, *supra* note 15; Amy Bradshaw, *supra* note 1.

law school to pursue social and economic justice stayed true to that goal, instead of less than a third, we'd be closer to achieving a shift in resources and a balancing of the scales of justice.

To pursue public interest law, civil rights, and justice for all, not only for those who can pay, but for everyone, can exact a great cost from the few who persevere toward social and economic justice. Yet, as with most heart-driven endeavors, the challenges are presented as invaluable lessons along the way, making the rewards of the work all the sweeter; gifts really, if one can become expansive enough to accept the intention of the gift-giver. And, the good news is that research on happiness has demonstrated that people who are primarily motivated by money are less happy and less healthy than those motivated in other ways.[37]

In addition, there are avenues over, around, and through the obstacles, as the stories of the lawyers in this chapter have shown. Until legal education undergoes drastic change and the road becomes easier, there are ways for individual law students to seek out the necessary support and guidance on the public interest law path. Psychically, seeking out like-minded public interest types and taking advantage of every public interest law program and opportunity in law school can sustain the passion from assault by the rest of the law school curriculum, a curriculum most unfriendly to public interest law concerns and issues. Finding professors passionate about justice issues and public interest law is possible in almost every law school, not just those on the public-interest-friendly radar. One study found that, in addition to entering law school with an intention to practice public interest law, the second strongest influence on pursuing that dream is working in a job related to public interest law during summer breaks.[38]

The best approach financially is to start planning early for a public interest law career; to realize that every dollar of debt will matter when graduating from law school and entering the public interest law field with the predictably low starting salaries. Finding

---

37. Jonathan Haidt, *supra* note 24 at 95.
38. McGill, *supra* note 1 at 702.

a state school with lower tuition, achieving scholarships at a private school, going to a law school with an LRAP, minimizing living expenses, working during school, and attending law school in a city with a lower cost of living are all ways of consciously lessening educational debt. Learn all you can about the federal LRAP and how to fall within its purview.[39] Working with the law school's financial aid office, law students need to be as aggressive about the financial aspects of their life as they are about their studies and other aspects of life. So many people end up realizing their debt load only during the exit interview with the financial aid office. The mantra "I wish I had paid more attention to the debt I was getting into" was repeated over and over in the interviews I held.

Once in the working world, there are a multitude of approaches to maintaining a comfortable lifestyle on a public interest law salary. One can pursue one of the fellowships available for public interest lawyers. And, even if not chosen as one of the fortunate few to receive a fellowship, choices exist that one can make to lessen the stress of low wages. It is important to again stress the value of creating an emotional support system of like-minded family and friends to help maintain motivation in work that is perceived as on the fringes of society. Espy and another lawyer I interviewed that we will meet later, Maria, were able to live with their parents for a short time to gain a financial foothold. Others found roommates and, although not their first choice of lifestyle, accepted shared living situations as viable alternatives to pursue their dreams of public interest law jobs. The rewards of doing so and staying true to your values can outweigh the inconvenience. In addition to pursuing the dream, everyone spoke of the collegiality and community of their offices of co-workers as a significant component in waking up each morning looking forward to going to work.

---

39. Michael Mulé reports that students must know to enroll in the Federal Consolidation Program (FCP) which is part of the U.S. Department of Education. You can only consolidate loans once so if you consolidate with another program you will be pre-empted out of the federal loan assistance program. Phone conversation, March 2008.

Positions at Legal Services offices outside of the major metropolitan areas are sometimes less competitive. Smaller cities often provide the advantage of a lower cost of living. As was the case with Jonathan Feldman, who moved to Rochester, New York, to be able to afford home ownership, considering various options of where to live might lead to greater financial flexibility (although his job at the Empire Justice Center was highly competitive). If need be, there might be opportunities for a second job, as in the case of Crystal Doody who found an undergraduate business school at which to teach law courses in the evening.

For the courageous few, determined to pursue work that feeds their passionate hearts and not their wallets, creative ways to accommodate lives on public interest wages are found and flexible budgets and lifestyles are maintained. It *can* be done. Lawyers *can* graduate from law school with mountains of educational debt and live comfortably, finding enormous reward and invaluable wealth in the work they love to wake up and go to each morning. Integrating mind, body, heart, and soul into the work we do happens in the lives of many public interest lawyers.

CHAPTER 5

A. THE WORK: ITS OWN REWARD

We've all heard the truisms about hard work and sacrifice leading to great rewards in life. My father's favorite was something like, "Deb, anything worth having is worth working your butt off for." In the case of public interest lawyers, working hard, earning enough to pay the bills, and keeping living expenses manageable leads to reaping the truest rewards of job satisfaction. The rewards of working day in and day out to improve the lives of people who wouldn't have had a chance for even subsistence needs without their public interest lawyers, making the world a better place one individual and whole communities of people at a time, are great. As you swim against the tide of a profession dominated by the quest for the powerful dollar, the profound nonmonetary rewards become easily apparent. When listening to that inner voice and guided by the heart, doing work that makes us feel good inside becomes an immeasurable reward.

For lawyers just starting out, or lawyers who've been fighting the good fight for decades, the nonmonetary rewards are what gets them out of bed in the morning, eager to get to work, and what helps them fall asleep at night after a day of meaningful work. This enthusiasm for the work is present from day one. Legal Services lawyers get to interact with clients, handle cases, and go to court (sometimes even federal court) from the first week on the job. They are not relegated to a back office, doing research, writing memos, and handling nonclient matters for partners and senior associates. Hitting the ground running, Legal Services lawyers experience the joy, pain, elation, fear, and incredible responsibility and privilege of lawyering from the start. One lawyer, who found these challenges and rewards in the first year of her public interest law career, is Pamela Kim.

Pamela Kim

Pamela Kim took a year off between completing her undergraduate work at Cornell University and beginning Northwestern Law School. During that year, she taught English in Korea. Describing herself as "technically" first generation American, Pamela explains that:

> My background is a little confusing. My parents were born and married in Korea and my dad's company placed him in their New York office so I just happened to be born in New York. I am an American citizen but when I was very young we then moved to Costa Rica so I actually grew up there. I went to an American private school there, graduated from high school there, and came back to the states for undergrad and law school. My family is still down in Costa Rica. My dad has a business down there. I'm here, by myself, doing my thing.

Pamela has known her "thing" would be public interest law since her spring semester at Cornell University when she enrolled in a Washington, DC program for Cornell students and "on a whim" decided to do the required externship at Amnesty International in DC. The work was "great and inspiring" and Pamela knew "from there, eventually, I didn't know if it was right after law school or what, but I knew eventually I wanted to go into non-profit work." She remembers:

> While I was there I really didn't have very many responsibilities. There was a lot of photocopying, a lot of stuffing envelopes, a lot of making phone calls, dropping folders off at centers and offices, things like that. So, it wasn't really anything too substantial, but just being around these people who firmly believed in everything they were doing and they made me feel like every photocopy I was making could change the world. That was the kind of environment and atmosphere I wanted to work in, where I feel like I'm making a difference. And even if it's something as small as a photocopy, people were really inspiring, people were really hopeful that change could happen. It was great to be working in that and that's where I wanted to be.

So, Pamela took a year off between undergraduate and law school to work and save money for law school. Living with relatives in Korea and teaching English, Pamela saved most of her salary for law school. Northwestern had accepted her and had given her a one-year deferred admission. Northwestern University had met Pamela's criteria for a law school, including living particularly in a big city, being a training ground for lawyers (not professors), and offering very strong clinical programs and a Center for Human Rights and the Family and Children Justice Center. The generous financial aid package they provided Pamela was a big factor in her decision to go to Northwestern, knowing it would significantly reduce the amount of money she would have to borrow. Pamela would be pleasantly surprised when she started at Northwestern to find out that they had a loan forgiveness program for graduates pursuing public interest law or government work.

Even with the generous scholarships, financial aid package, and money Pamela had saved from her year teaching in Korea, she graduated law school in May 2005 $80,000 in educational debt. Not swayed from her commitment to public interest law, Pamela worked at the Legal Aid Foundation during her law school summers and sought out the minority of students who similarly did not waver from their public interest law path. Pamela remembers that there were a lot of students interested in public interest law but "for whatever reason, I don't know if it was the external pressure or financial reasons or whatever, I know there were a lot of people who chose to say, 'Well, I'm going to go to a law firm right after law school and then maybe after a few years, after I've paid down my debt, I'll go back to my original interest in public interest law.'" The pressure at Northwestern from big-firm recruiters is intense because it is a top 15 law school. Most students end up going to the big firms and Pamela remembers that, when asked what they were doing for the summer after their second year of law school, "it was, 'I'm going to Sidley Austin, I'm going to Skadden, I'm going to Kirkland and Ellis.' And, there I was, 'Oh, I'm going to the Legal Assistance Foundation.'" The part-time person dedicated to public interest law in the career services office is "wonderful" according to Pamela and "has a lot of connections, especially within the Chicago public interest community. She's worked in public interest but she's only part-time." Pamela would recommend that Northwestern invest in a full-time public interest career advisor to balance the overwhelming emphasis on private sector employment.

Despite the odds and her educational debt, Pamela stays true to her dream sparked at Amnesty International to be a part of changing the world. With monthly loan payments of more than $800 and a starting salary of $41,000 a year in Chicago, Pamela has not regretted her determination and decision. She lives in a small apartment, by herself, with rent of $710 a month, in a lower cost area than a lot of her friends who work at law firms and live by Lake Michigan. She takes public transportation and, except for grocery shopping, doesn't mind not having a car. Watching every penny (literally), Pamela says, "I keep track of my budget very carefully. I use money management software. It's downloading from my bank statements online so I can see exactly where my money's going." Northwestern's LRAP helps but Pamela says:

> I don't know if I'm being overly idealistic or overestimating my budgeting skills but I've been eyeing my budget and even with having to make payments of $800 every month I've still been managing to break even, even without the loan forgiveness grant. That's what I've been trying to shoot for just in case, for whatever reason, something happens and I need money for a rainy day. That's what I've been shooting for and that's sort of where I've been hovering.

The loan forgiveness program helped Pamela financially her first year after law school with a lump sum of $5,000. Although based on and targeted for educational debt, the payment has no restrictions once paid to the recipient. Because a substantial portion of her loans are private and she has a 20-year payment plan with variable interest, Pamela is trying to pay that off as quickly as possible. With help from the LRAP, her budgeting skills, and determination, she has even been able to save a little money. But, as she says, there are trade-offs:

> I think it's doable. It's not easy. There's been a lot of things I've had to give up. I hardly buy clothes. The suits that I own are the suits that I bought when I was doing on-campus interviewing. It's difficult. I don't go out to eat very much. I try to bring my lunch when I can. Even when I do go out to eat with my friends I try to make sure it's a place I can afford. I'm pretty up front with my friends about the fact that I have a lot of

127

debt, that I can't afford to go places and everybody's been very respectful of that.

Pamela credits her upbringing, life circumstances, and unknown forces in giving her the drive and commitment to live her values:

> I guess part of it is because I do feel like I've been very fortunate in my own experience. My parents could afford to send me to a private school in Costa Rica. I don't necessarily know where this came from, but it's sort of this feeling that I want to give back to other people who haven't been as fortunate. I did see it a lot in Costa Rica. There is a lot of poverty; it's still a developing country, although its standard of living is much higher than other Central American countries. Also, coming back to the states and seeing how everybody else's experiences as immigrants or as minorities kind of come into play, that was also a big factor for me in wanting to help people who are disadvantaged because of circumstances that are out of their control.

Finally, Pamela knows how much happier and satisfied in her career she is than her friends at private firms. She says:

> Everything that I've given up in terms of material gain or material possessions, it has been more than compensated by the fact that I'm happy doing my job versus a lot of my friends in law firms who are worked to the bone for the money they need. They make a lot of money but it comes at a cost. They work long hours and they work long hours at things that I don't necessarily find exciting. I get to go to court, I get to argue motions, I get to have a ton of client contact and a lot of my friends in law firms never meet the clients or, if they go to court once a month on

something the partner thinks is routine enough for them to handle, they're lucky.

I've learned so much. I've gotten a lot of really great experience. I work with great groups of people. I really enjoy the connections that I'm making with my clients. That's why I definitely feel part of the job; I actually get to talk with real people and get to actually see how what I'm doing affects their lives. For me, it's definitely been worth it and I would hope that more people would choose to do it even if it is a little bit difficult financially.

B. LIVING AN AUTHENTIC LIFE

At the other end of the career spectrum is Michael Deutsch, who remains inspired and motivated as a civil rights lawyer after more than three decades of practicing public interest law. Also having practiced public interest law for more than 30 years is someone I interviewed who wished to remain anonymous, and wanted to be referred to as "Art." Michael Deutsch and Art have been through the challenges and struggles of public interest lawyering, stayed true to their heartfelt passion about the work, and have careers they can reflect on with pride and gratitude.

Michael Deutsch

Michael Deutsch continues to engage in social, economic, and political justice lawyering after 35 years of dedicating his life to representing defendants unjustly accused; prisoners, mostly political prisoners, denied even the most basic of rights; and people on death row having confessed to crimes they did not commit after being brutally tortured by the Chicago police department. He remains tireless, dedicated, creative, and determined to use his brilliant mind to uphold the most moral and ethical principles of justice and the law for the benefit of those who would not otherwise have access to fundamental rights, let alone fairness and justice. In his early

129

60s now, Michael reflects back on his life's work at a time when the hard-fought freedoms under this country's Constitution are being threatened with a severity unparalleled in recent history. When we spoke in July 2007, he said:

> If you measure it in terms of lasting change, look at where we are in human rights, constitutional rights, we're in a bad situation with a lot of things. The Supreme Court is moving to the right. I think it's just one vote away from disaster really. Even though there are these little victories that happen. I would say that on good days I feel like what I've done is meaningful and important and I've made a contribution. On not so good days I say, what have I done? What have I changed? What permanent things are better because I've spent all this time fighting these fights? That's part of anybody, not just lawyers, but anybody who's really chosen a path of human rights or political rights or justice. It's not easy. You see that you're not always in the mainstream and you have to deal with that. You're on the fringes.

The fringes are a much better place because of Michael Deutsch. No matter what the challenges in retrospect or in looking ahead, Michael knows he couldn't be doing anything else; he couldn't be in the private sector "really, essentially, making the system work better for the rich people."

A product of the civil and political rights era, Michael graduated from Northwestern University Law School in 1969. Having been second in his class after the first year, he received full scholarships for his second and third years of law school. The educational success he experienced in law school was a surprise to Michael; he had initially been wait-listed. His undergraduate grades at the University of Illinois were not great. But, for some reason, he had a superior "knack" for writing law school exams. The ability to be tops in his class and receive the scholarships meant that Michael graduated without debt. A child of a working-class family, Michael was on his own financially in law school and would have had to take out loans if not for the full scholarships.

When he graduated from law school, Michael clerked for a U.S. Court of Appeals Judge in the Seventh Circuit. Michael had become politicized in law school "particularly because of the war in Viet Nam." He says:

> I also got involved in the counterculture movement, thinking about how this whole life is too materialistic, we should live a more simple life and we should love everyone. Those kinds of things began to politicize me while I was in law school. The assassination of Martin Luther King happened in 1967, those kinds of events, the assassination of Robert Kennedy, who I thought might be a good presidential candidate. By the time I was getting out of law school I was very political. What happened was because I was eligible for the draft I had an option to work for a federal judge, which gave me a draft deferment. That was one of the impetuses that caused me to decide to become a law clerk for a federal judge.

During law school Michael had decided that he would, in his words "use my skills to help people who were fighting for a better society, for justice." Then when he was clerking for the Seventh Circuit appellate judge on the 27th floor of the federal building in Chicago, the Chicago conspiracy trial was taking place on the 20th floor.[40] The more he observed the trial, the more he wanted to

---

40. The Chicago Seven conspiracy trial began on September 24, 1969, and involved seven men, including Abbie Hoffman, Tom Hayden, and Jerry Rubin, accused of conspiring to incite a riot at the 1968 Democratic National Convention held in Chicago. They were represented by William Kunstler and Leonard Weinglass. Five of the seven men were convicted of violating the Anti-Riot Act of 1968 and two were acquitted after the trial that lasted until February 18, 1970. The five convictions were appealed and the 7th Circuit Court of Appeals reversed the convictions of all five men on November 21, 1972 (www.law.umkc.edu/faculty/projects/trials/Chicago7.html).

practice law the way the defense attorneys were practicing law. He had been getting to know the lawyers who founded the People's Law Office and, wanting to work with like-minded people and take on cases he believed in, he left the federal clerkship and went to work for the People's Law Office. The new firm had been created in 1969 and Michael joined in 1970. He describes the firm this way: "It began as a storefront law office and was initially created because people felt there was an important need to represent activists who were protesting the war and racism in the country. Particularly, a lot of people were being arrested, both Black Panthers, Young Lords, which was a Puerto Rican political organization, and the antiwar protesters." Michael left the judicial clerkship specifically drawn to a high-profile case the law office had taken in Carbondale, Illinois, involving a Black Panther chapter. Their house had been surrounded by police, a shootout had occurred, and five of the residents were charged with 47 counts of attempted murder. In Michael's first trial ever, lasting more than eight weeks, a verdict of 47 counts of not guilty was returned by the jury. Michael and the other lawyer on the case and two law students lived in a big farmhouse in Carbondale with a collective of people during the time they prepared for and went to trial. Sharing the rent and one car and living very simply, they supported themselves by representing defendants accused of minor drug charges, as he recalls, "hippies and students" arrested mostly for marijuana possession.

After the verdict in the Black Panther trial, the defense team rewarded themselves with a camping trip to the Ozarks. Wondering how he would ever top the success of his first trial, Michael did not have to wonder for long. Coming out of the woods into the nearest town, they saw newspaper headlines that read "Prisoners Take Over Attica Prison."[41] Arriving in Buffalo, New York (the

---

41. The Attica prison was taken over by 1,300 inmates in September 1971. After negotiations failed on their demands involving living conditions and access to education and training, then Governor Rockefeller ordered the state police and the National Guard to seize the prison. This action resulted in the death of 43 individuals, including 10 of the prison guards the inmates had been holding hostage. "Attica Revisited," *Talking History Project*, available at www.talkinghistory.org/attica.

largest city near Attica) just a couple of weeks after the takeover, Michael would spend the next eight years or so commuting between Chicago and Buffalo in two-month intervals. He explains the work, saying:

> We were doing several things. We were representing the prisoners around their treatment right after the retaking of the prison. A lot of the leaders were put in isolation. We were trying to get them out of isolation. We were challenging their administrative detention. We were trying to get people medical treatment who hadn't gotten it yet. We were trying to interview people, understanding that there was going to probably be criminal charges, and we were trying to set up some kind of structure that would serve as a support and defense committee for the Attica prisoners. I was doing legal work but also political work, organizing work, trying to organize lawyers from other places to come.

Back in Chicago, at the People's Law Office, Michael would spend the two months on litigating class action suits on prisoners' rights cases, especially around the isolation units that were beginning to be utilized in the early 1970s; representing plaintiffs in police brutality cases; and doing general criminal defense work. A case Michael was handling involved a peaceful protest against brutality at Marion Federal Prison in Illinois. New law was made when the Seventh Circuit Court of Appeals upheld the lower court's ruling that the time in the segregation unit suffered by about 25 percent of the prisoners involved in the peaceful protest, almost 18 months, was a disproportionate punishment in violation of the Eighth Amendment of the Constitution. Prison officials tried to get around the ruling by classifying certain prisoners in need of special housing based on their conviction, rather than as a consequence of specific behavior. The People's Law

Office attorneys had subsequent victories challenging these practices.

Ultimately, the Attica work was extraordinarily victorious. The Attica Brothers had been facing serious murder charges. As Michael recalls:

> We stopped the criminal prosecutions and ultimately everybody got clemency from that and that was politically successful. So, it was like you took off at a whirlwind. You stepped on it and it just took you and you never really looked back. You thought, "Wow, this is great. What I'm doing is great. I love the people I'm meeting. This is just what I should be doing." So, I never really had second thoughts at that period, "Oh, why am I doing this? I'm suffering so much." It was all positive for me.

These sentiments prevailed despite the financial hardship Michael was enduring at the time. In his words:

> I didn't make any money in Buffalo. The law office was supporting us. The office was in bad financial shape and I remember I had some money that I had saved literally from being a law clerk because I had made, at that time it seemed like a lot of money, about $14,000 as a law clerk. I had some money and I was using that money and we were getting a little stipend each week from the law office. I remember having to go around to friends during that period asking them to lend me some money and borrowing money to keep going. It was tough times in terms of money, but again, I was single, I didn't have any responsibility, I didn't have any debt so I was able to get along all right on that.

When asked what sustained him then and what sustains him now, Michael responds:

> I would say, without sounding too Pollyannaish, I think what sustained me were my clients. I was blown away by the Attica brothers. There were a lot of them who were older than me; a lot of them were politically sophisticated. They had gone through this incredible rebellion and repression. They had seen their brothers killed in front of them. They had been beaten and tortured and yet they still had this tremendous strength of character and resistance. I felt like if they could do that then certainly I could commit myself to helping them knowing full well that I had the luxury to quit or say that it was too hard and go back to some other thing, but they didn't.

The Attica saga would not end until 1999. The criminal cases would be dismissed and in 1974 a civil lawsuit was brought on behalf of the estates of the inmates who had been killed and the survivors who had been beaten and tortured. The case would continue for 25 years until a settlement for $12 million was agreed to. By then, many lawyers had been involved and the $3 million in attorney's fees was split many ways.

In the midst of the Attica defense, during one of his return trips to Chicago, Michael met another inspiring client who had been a political prisoner since 1954. Rafael Cancel Miranda was in the federal prison in Marion, Illinois, when Michael met him. Rafael had spent a lot of time in Alcatraz. Through Rafael, Michael would learn about inhumane treatment of the Puerto Rican nationalists who had been in prison for more than 20 years. With one other lawyer, Michael brought a class action lawsuit on behalf of the Puerto Rican nationalists and the independence movement. Their demands were for basic rights — the right to have visitors in prison and to have access to literature — that were being denied to them.

The lawsuit was won and an international campaign for the release of the prisoners was strengthened by the victory. Michael's clients had not sought their own release, yet in 1979 they were granted unconditional release by then President Jimmy Carter. Michael remembers, "I accompanied them back to Puerto Rico and there were just tens of thousands of people at the airport. I traveled through the island with them."

When the FALN, an underground Puerto Rican independence group, started claiming responsibility for bombings in Chicago and New York City, many of the people Michael had become friends with through his representation of the Puerto Rican nationalists came under intense scrutiny. It was the early 1980s and Michael fought many of the grand jury investigations and indictments. When someone associated with the FALN was in an apartment building in Queens that was destroyed by a bomb, survived the explosion, and was charged with possession of explosives, Michael went to represent him in federal court in Brooklyn. Michael's client insisted that the court had no jurisdiction over him because he was an independence fighter and as such a prisoner of war. Over the judge's objections, Michael argued international law, the right to resist, and prisoner of war status for his client. The jury in federal court convicted the defendant. In the meantime, many political activists calling for Puerto Rican independence were being indicted under suspicion of being connected with the FALN. When the activists refused to testify before a federal grand jury, they were indicted for criminal contempt. The government requested sentences of 15 years for them but the judge gave them two- to three-year sentences after they had already spent 18 months in prison.

Michael interjects, "Along the way I got married." He remembers it to be 1979 or 1980. His first wife had a 7-year-old daughter Michael adopted; the financial pressures became intense. He says, "Now I had some financial situations and I was always uptight about money. My wife was finishing school to become a school teacher, but she wasn't able to work yet, and I remember worrying and being in debt and thinking about how I was going to pay this one and that one and always being behind in terms of money." But he never considered doing anything else. He says, "It was too all encompassing. It was too fulfilling. It was too interesting and I never thought that maybe I should get a job in a corporate law firm." And he remembers being able to put it in perspective, thinking, "When you see people who are really suffering, people who are living in prison or living in real poverty you say. 'Gee, it's not so bad for me.' I didn't really sacrifice too much I don't think." Michael's first marriage did not end due to the financial pressures. It was mostly the demands of the job and the travel involved, including almost five years of living in Hartford, Connecticut, defending about 20 people who were arrested in Puerto Rico and accused of conspiracy to rob Wells Fargo of $7 million in the name of Puerto Rican independence.

After Michael and his first wife divorced, Michael moved to New York City and became the legal director of the Center for Constitutional Rights (CCR). During his time at CCR, from 1992 to 1996, he handled a variety of cases, including representing homeless people who had been arrested at Pennsylvania Station, a major railroad and subway station in New York City. There were also cases against generals from Haiti, Guatemala, and Indonesia being sued in U.S. courts for violating international law by torturing U.S. citizens in their countries. Michael was involved in years of preparation for a civil trial against the FBI for false arrest and defamation of a woman who was a leader of Earth First in California. A bomb had been planted in her car and it blew up, seriously injuring her. She was then falsely convicted of carrying a bomb. As she lay in her hospital bed after the bomb exploded, the FBI had her chained to the bed. The local criminal charges were eventually dropped due to lack of evidence, but CCR brought a civil case and after trial got her a $4 million verdict. Unfortunately, the award went to her estate. Tragically, she had died of breast cancer before the trial. Another case brought by CCR that Michael was involved in was against Unicol, a multinational corporation that had built a pipeline in Burma with the help of the Burmese army, enslaving local people and forcing them to work on the pipeline against their will. That case settled for a lot of money due to the culpability of the corporation and the severity of the injustice.

In addition, throughout this time, the Attica civil case was still ongoing. The trial had occurred in 1991 and 1992 but there were appeals, attempts to settle, and a lot of work at the Court of Appeals level. Michael's salary at CCR was only $42,000 a year as the legal director, so he arranged to spend 20 percent of his time on federally appointed counsel cases. Financially, Michael remembers, "I was probably making more money than I ever made at the People's Law Office. Again, I didn't have a car and I didn't go on vacations, but it was all right. I did have financial responsibilities for my daughter, who was now at the University of Chicago as an undergraduate, and also there was money in the divorce, but it was alright. I was able to do okay at that point."

In 1996 Michael left CCR and moved back to Chicago, having met his present wife, who works at the People's Law Office in Chicago. Working out of his house for a while, doing some writing and part-time lawyering, Michael didn't return to the People's Law Office until about 1998. Since then Michael has worked on mostly big, challenging, time-consuming, impact cases saying, "I always tried to avoid taking cases that you do over and over again. The thing that interests me is trying to be creative as a lawyer and trying to use the law to deal with political legal situations." One of these situations is the case in Indiana of a man who's been convicted of a crime punishable by the death penalty. Michael explains:

> He's already been convicted of it but his death sentence has been set aside twice so they want to give him a third death penalty trial 25 years after his conviction. All his mitigation witnesses are dead, evidence has disappeared, plus the jury is going to know that if they don't give him death he is going to come out in five years because at the time he committed his crime the alternative to death in Indiana was 60 years and you do 30. So he's only got five more years to do if he doesn't get death, which is a tough choice because he's convicted of killing a policeman in the course of a bank robbery.

Michael has argued the case twice in the Indiana Supreme Court and has had two trials, the last of which ended with the judge prohibiting the death penalty out of a sense of fairness because too much time had gone by. Michael quotes the judge, who had just come back from serving as a Lieutenant Colonel in Iraq, as saying, "Even though I think the crime he committed is horrible, I'm not going to allow him to have a death trial because it would violate fairness and due process." The state appealed the ruling.

Another case Michael has been working on extensively for at least two years is that of a Palestinian man who lives in the United States. In 1993 he was arrested in Israel and charged with financially aiding the Hamas resistance. After being tortured and interrogated for three months, he confessed and spent five years in prison in Israel. After his release and return to the United States, he was designated a "special terrorist" by the federal government, which denied him the rights to spend or receive money without a license. In 2004 he was indicted in the United States for his actions and confession in Israel in 1993 and charged under the RICO statute.[42] Michael is defending this father of five in what he terms a "political persecution." And, because it's post-9/11, and the government can classify all the evidence against Michael's client, Michael cannot even cross-examine the Israeli interrogators about the methods they used to obtain his client's confession. The methods of physical and psychological pressure that the interrogators used in 1993 were outlawed by the Israeli Supreme Court in 1999 as torture. But still, Michael cannot question them on how they extracted the confession from his client.[43]

Similarly, in Chicago, Michael works with other lawyers at the People's Law Office on bringing to light the history and pattern of torture of African-American men by the Chicago police force that

---

42. The Racketeer Influenced and Corrupt Organizations Act provides for increased penalties for persons convicted of crimes connected to racketeering and criminal organizations. RICO Act, 18 U.S.C. §§ 1961-1968.

43. As an update, "In February, 2007, in a stunning victory, Muhammad Salah was acquitted of the major charge against him concerning terrorism conspiracy and convicted only of a minor obstruction charge for answering interrogatories in a civil case." Michael Deutsch, e-mail message to author, October 10, 2007.

went on unabated from the 1970s through the 1990s. At least four men were released from death row and from prison after their confessions were proven to have resulted from torture at the hands of the police.

In his early 60s now, with two young children, and his wife working part-time at the People's Law Office so she can be home for the kids after school, Michael does not see retirement in his future. He's very matter-of-fact about it and says:

> I never worried about having enough money to retire. I just felt like all these other people are struggling and fighting for justice, are in prison or facing prison, they're not worried about the money for retiring so I'm not going to structure my life based on being able to have a pension and retire. Maybe when I get to be an age I'll say, "Oh my God, I wish I had a retirement fund," but that's just the price you pay for doing this kind of work.

And, he reflects:

> The question that I have is how do these lawyers who've been working at these big corporate law firms for 30, 35 years keep doing it, because really, the pay-off is really money, that's all it is. Maybe they do some pro-bono work, and some of them do, that makes them happy. But, my work is all that way so I don't really have that much to complain about in that regard.

Despite the reversal of many of the political and legal victories Michael has won over the years, despite the prison conditions now, and the increased threat to constitutional rights for us all, Michael does think his work has been meaningful. He's very proud of being an integral part of building the People's Law Office and he says, "That's something that I think we've created and built all these years. I think it's an institution that we established which is something that we can look back on, and say that we did that. People know us in the city and they respect us. Judges might not like us but they know that we're going to do competent, creative legal work."

As for advice for people coming out of law school nowadays, Michael's experience and wisdom capture the essence of the struggle:

I would tell them to get involved with some people who are doing work that they believe in. What seems meaningful to them, what they feel passionate about, because in the end I think the passion about your work is really what's most important. Obviously, they have to pay their debts and support their family and that's a big problem. But I've seen too many people say that and go into some kind of corporate world and never be able to come out. You just fill that lifestyle in and your debts never go away because you need more things and you need better and nicer houses, and nice cars and better vacations. You look around and you're 40 or 50 and you've spent all your time helping rich people become richer. So, I think it's really worthwhile while you're in law school to even volunteer in some law firm or public interest group that does things that you really believe in and see how you really feel about doing that. There's always ways to pay your bills and figure it out. Nobody's going to come and arrest you for your debt. I would just encourage them not to just say, "I have all this debt so I really don't want to do this but I'm going to work for this corporate law firm." I think your passions will be quickly diminished and you'll forget why you went to law school if you did go for political reasons or social justice reasons.

Michael Deutsch's incredible public interest law career spanning three decades exists as a testament to the rewards of soulful lawyering. He's handled the most difficult and challenging civil rights cases of those decades, seen many successes, and seen some erosion of the gains in civil rights work over the years. His commitment has been unwavering. Although he might humbly question his accomplishments, he never questions his dedication.

The next example of the long-haul dedication and priceless rewards of public interest lawyering is a civil rights attorney who handles mostly fair housing and discrimination cases in New York State and has done so for 30 years. This attorney chose to be called "Art."

Art (pseudonym)

To say that Art is understated is an understatement in itself. Art is a national fair housing resource. He litigates the most challenging housing discrimination cases, has met with Department of Housing and Urban Development (HUD) officials, has submitted written testimony to Congressional committees, and has written lengthy articles for trade and law journals. He's also just a really nice person. He could be very full of himself, yet he is so reserved and unassuming, he didn't even want his real name used for this book.

After graduating from a small midwestern law school he attended because it was in a rural area and the idea of going off to nowhere and studying law appealed to him, Art moved to the Pacific Northwest as a VISTA lawyer. He worked for an Indian services organization designed to provide social services and legal assistance to an Indian tribe for which federal assistance had been terminated. His primary motivation was doing work that he would enjoy rather than trying to make a lot of money.

With little direction when he decided to apply for law school, he describes his original motivation in this way: "I assumed that whatever I wanted to do I would do more effectively with a law degree." He was interested in special education and thought that a law degree would benefit his ability to advocate for children in the special education arena quickly adding, "I also had a friend who was a Seneca Indian, and I got interested in Indian law issues just before

I went to school and while I was in law school. I started dabbling with Indian law issues and got interested in the VISTA program to work with an Indian government."

The concept of public interest law had not yet developed when Art went to law school at the end of the 1960s revolution. Civil rights activists were gravitating toward pragmatic change and social justice strategy was evolving from protesting to advocating for civil rights. Art remembers that law schools hadn't adjusted yet and most did not have clinics or public interest programs. The activist students at his law school, including Art, initiated the creation of the first clinic at the law school. With the support of a faculty advisor, the students developed a criminal justice clinic as the first clinical course.

Art worked for the Indian organization from August 1975 until the end of 1976. The VISTA stipend at that time was $221 a month and the lawyers received $50 a month in food stamps. Student loan payments were suspended during the duration of the VISTA volunteer period and, because Art graduated from law school with $12,000 in debt in 1975, when new cars cost about $3,000 and a new house in upstate New York was about $25,000, the grace period was a significant benefit, but payments under the loan programs were not forgiven for VISTA volunteers, just suspended. Art figures that $12,000 in debt at that time would be equivalent to about $100,000 in debt now because it represented three times the cost of a new car and half the cost of a new house.

The lifestyle of the VISTA lawyers was not as stark as their meager salaries would indicate. Art remembers that "in those days the theory was that you should learn to live the way your clients live. They were poor and you should understand their problems." There was a significant distinction between the lives of the clients and the lives of the VISTA lawyers, however, in that the VISTA lawyers had what Art characterizes as "intellectual resources" and cultural advantages. He recalls five of his colleagues who pooled their stipends and were able to rent a luxury house with air conditioning and a swimming pool. Art found an apartment in the small city where he was assigned that "was as big as a phone booth" but it was nice and clean and the rent was $94 a month, or half of his stipend. VISTA granted an allowance at the end of the volunteer period so Art left with a check for about $600. He decided to return home to New York State and found a job in a rural legal services office in January 1977 for his first paying job.

Coming from the VISTA position, Art was starting from scratch in terms of setting up a house and buying a car. His starting annual salary at Legal Services was $11,000. The cost of living was fairly low in this rural area, but he did find it advantageous to share a house. Reflecting back, Art has this insight: "It's funny, I always found that whatever salary increases I got, I spent as much as I made. I wasn't saving a lot. For some reason I saved more when I was with VISTA. When you get that first job you do things like buy a stereo, buy a camera, and buy a used car. So I sort of spent what I got and didn't save much." And, Art was making his first school loan payments to the tune of around $100 a month with a ten-year term.

In mid-1979, Art moved to an urban area in New York to start work at another legal services program. His starting salary there was $19,000 a year. Again spending as much as he made, he nonetheless was able to pay his bills without any problem. Then in 1982 when he acquired a position with the state legal services support center, he moved to another upstate city in New York, and started earning $32,000 a year. Art marveled at the amount of income: "Compared to all my Legal Services' colleagues I thought this was an embarrassment of riches." By this point, Art was a veteran legal services attorney, and with seven years of practice to his credit, one of the most experienced. Legal Services had been created in 1974, so by the late 1970s the attorneys who began at Legal Services offices with one or two years of experience were veterans. Art's bosses had to convince him that, with seven years of experience, he was a seasoned attorney and he deserved the salary they were offering.

Turning 32 years old and being the unique person he is, Art finally realized he needed to think about his long-term economic security. His immediate concern was a desire to buy a house, but he also realized he needed to think about savings and investments due to the lack of any pension at Legal Services. In the early 1980s, real estate market interest rates were near 15 percent. Art thought he had found the bargain of the century when he was able to buy a seller-financed home at a 12 percent interest rate. He was also very aware that buying a house would have been a lot more challenging, if not impossible, if he were still a Legal Services attorney and not being paid the higher salary afforded by the state support center. Now that home ownership was a reality, he realized he was going to have to take it upon himself to save for retirement. Not having the added financial concerns of a family, Art has been able to save for retirement and has been a strong advocate within Legal Services for a pension plan for the attorneys. He understands that most Legal Services attorneys devote their lives to helping poor people and really don't care how much money they make as long as they can take care of their families and have economic security. He reflects:

> As we used to say, "Don't become our own clients." There's a fear among Legal Services attorneys that if you're only working and paying your bills you're going to be 60 or 65 and you might have to retire because of physical problems and if you don't have anything but Social Security at that time or if you're dependent on SSI you literally become your own client. At one point I actually had a former attorney come into Legal Services and I thought, "Hmm, this really can happen." This guy was on SSI and only a government support check away from homelessness.

Art would like Legal Services programs to find a way to provide pension benefits for attorneys who are committed to the work for the long term. He's working hard within his office, advocating for a model plan that can be replicated in offices throughout the state.

C. COLLEGIALITY AND COLLABORATION

Lawyers working for the public good experience a collegiality and cooperativeness unparalleled in the legal profession. When monetary profit is not the motivating force, civility and professionalism can reign as paramount in the workplace. Echoed over and over in my interviews was the sentiment that people truly enjoyed going to the office for the work that lie ahead and also to see the people they work with, the people who've become friends in the tireless quest for justice and equality. Sue Augustus has been feeling this invaluable benefit of public interest lawyering over a span of decades and in many settings. She has felt the satisfaction of staying true to her ideal of using her law degree to help others. Both Sue and "Maria," whose story appears after Sue's, detoured briefly along their legal career paths into private law firms. They both realized their hearts and their homes were in public interest lawyering; that the rewards of public interest work were far greater than any salary a private firm could offer them.

Sue Augustus

Sue Augustus has practiced public interest law all but two of the years since she graduated from Chicago-Kent College of Law in 1982. She describes those two years of private practice as a "very slight detour." For the last four years, Sue has been the director of the Illinois state office for the Corporation for Supportive Housing (CSH), a national not-for-profit corporation that has offices in nine states. CSH distributes funding in the form of loans and grants to not-for-profit organizations that create housing for people who are homeless and disabled. Reflecting on the work of CSH, Sue says:

> I've worked with the same population for 24 years just with different legal issues. In some ways it's sad that not a whole lot has changed for really poor people. But it's fulfilling for me to be able to continue to do the work that I do. I'm not doing legal work now but we're trying to create housing for people who are getting out of prison to try and keep them out of prison, for people on SSI, for people who are home-less, and I've represented all those people. It was

interesting, when I was doing SSI work we were sitting around and saying, "You know, it would be so good if these people had case managers and someone to help them make sure they paid their bills and stayed in their apartment." And that's what supportive housing is. I think it's a really good solution for people who are poor and have other challenges like serious mental illness, chronic substance abuse, some chronic health conditions, where they just can't manage to keep their apartment without having someone give them some assistance. So, it's subsidized, affordable housing with services. I believe in the model and the mission of the organization. I don't know how long I'll be here, but I'll always be doing public interest work.

Judging from her legal career of more than two-and-a-half decades, Sue's commitment to public interest work is strong and adventurous. After graduating from the University of Notre Dame, Sue took a year and a half off from school and worked for a judge in Skokie, Illinois, officially on the payroll of the Cook County Sheriff's Department. Both a secretary and driver for the presiding judge, she was able to observe the criminal justice system and was struck by the inefficiency of the lawyers representing people accused of crimes. Sue decided to go to law school to pursue criminal defense work. Sue found an outlet for her interest in the law clinic at Chicago-Kent; she enrolled in the clinic in the second semester of her first year, and continued to work throughout her law school years, including actual court appearances in her last year of law school under a student practice order. The cases Sue worked on included the trial of 12 defendants charged with various crimes arising out of a prison riot in a state prison in the late 1970s. Because it was a very high-profile case, every time she went to court, Sue worked with 12 defendants, about 20 lawyers, and many law students. Of the case, Sue says, "The defendants were acquitted of all their crimes after trial. It was really a great experience."

Building on her law school experience, Sue worked for the State Appellate Defenders Office for five and a half years after graduating law school. Of the job, Sue remembers, "It was a very low-paying state job but it was a great job because we did appeals for people who had been convicted of crimes and couldn't afford a lawyer, so we were a public defender doing appeals. In the first two years I was out of law school I argued in the Illinois Supreme Court four times. It was just a great job for appellate work and learning a lot about the criminal justice system." All along, she was motivated by the work, not the paycheck, even though she had graduated from law school $25,000 in debt in 1982. With a salary of about $16,000, her loan payments were significant. Sue remembers:

> I budgeted myself so that I made sure I paid back my law school loans and my rent. I didn't have much left over but I was young and I didn't have a lot of other expenses. I had a car that would break down and my grandmother gave me her car so I didn't have a car payment. It was a time where I didn't have a lot of extra money. I made sure I paid that loan off every month. It took me ten years and I did it.

Along the way, Sue also co-founded Deborah's Place, a supportive housing project for women who are homeless. As the founding president when it was created 21 years ago, Sue has helped Deborah's Place become a premier permanent housing provider of its kind.

Now, at 50 years of age, Sue has no regrets in life. From those first years practicing criminal defense law, she went on to be the supervising attorney for a disability and elder law project at the Legal Aid Society of Dayton, Ohio (after those two forgettable years in private practice). She stayed there for five years and then, moving back to Chicago, supervised the adult SSI Advocacy Project at the Legal Assistance Foundation. By then it was 1996 and Congress passed legislation prohibiting Legal Services offices receiving federal funds from doing welfare reform work. Sue was among the attorneys at the Legal Assistance Foundation in Chicago who left that office to continue working on welfare reform and advocacy, joining another attorney to work at the SSI Coalition. During the six years she worked at the SSI Coalition, Sue represented people on issues regarding their SSI and Medicaid, helped file three class actions challenging the provisions dealing with SSI in the welfare reform law, and traveled around the country training other lawyers in how to help clients maintain their public benefits when returning to work.

Of the lifestyle trade-offs she's made to continue to live on public interest salaries, Sue says, "I don't feel like I'm really wanting for anything. I don't feel like I've given up a lot." The nonmonetary rewards sustain Sue.

> I never really thought of doing anything else. I tried the private practice. It just wasn't for me, chasing people down for money. Working for a not-for-profit makes me feel good. I like the work that I do. I have benefits so I don't worry about insurance. The camaraderie that comes from working in a place where everyone's there because they want to help other people is, I think, what keeps me going. Usually, I have so enjoyed the people that I've worked with that it's hard to leave a job because I leave behind so many friends. So, that's really what sustains me. I never had any interest in making huge sums of money or working a hundred hours a week.

Sue credits nature, not nurture, for her commitment to social justice. "There's no tradition of public service or even any Democrats in my family. I wasn't raised to be this way; I was born this way." For others wanting to pursue a similar path, Sue mentions the supports that are in place now that didn't even exist when she graduated law school, such as loan forgiveness programs and public interest fellowships. As she says, "I think that if you're committed to this kind of work you'll figure out a way to do it, and if you're not then it's easy to say that you'll just go and make the big money. If you have an interest in it and you don't seize it right away it will be hard to get it back. That's my best advice, and it can be done."

Maria

Maria was born in Mexico. Her family of seven immigrated to the United States when Maria was six years old. They settled in Washington Heights, a New York City neighborhood in transition when they arrived. It became predominantly poor with all the attendant social problems of poverty. Her father, a medical doctor in Mexico, had to redo his residency in the United States. Maria's mother didn't speak any English when they first arrived in the United States. Maria and her sisters and brother had to translate for her mother, and being noticeably Mexican, they experienced what she gently characterizes as "not nice behavior."

There is an air of serenity around Maria as she relates the story of her childhood, the discrimination her family endured, and the challenges of growing up "in a tough neighborhood, in tough schools." The strength of conviction and character born from the struggles of those formative years exude from Maria. She is quietly intense as she discloses that she always knew she wanted to do public interest work and she credits her unique growing up and background with that desire. It was her parents' insistence on the value of education that saved Maria and her siblings from the less fortunate fates some of the kids she grew up with endured. It was the firsthand experience of what happens to kids who grow up receiving public assistance, without opportunity to escape the cycle of poverty, that compelled Maria to continue to law school after graduating from college. "I wanted to do something meaningful and something . . . something good with my life . . . and that's why I wanted to go."

Maria went to Fordham University for undergraduate school and, despite having a scholarship, needed to take out loans. Her parents helped as much as they could with college tuition but there were five kids in the family and, wanting them all to have the benefit of higher education, the family's resources did not go far. Maria was forced to take out loans to pay for the remaining costs. When deciding on law school, she first narrowed her geographical choice to New York City, and then chose to attend NYU rather than Columbia University because NYU had more public interest opportunities, including clinical courses and an LRAP for graduates pursuing public interest law. Maria graduated law school in 1992 when the LRAP at NYU was not as generous as it is now, but it did help her out for a couple of years. Graduating with about $100,000 of educational debt, Maria has been paying about $800 a month on school loan repayment.

With a 20-year loan payoff period looming before her, Maria made the difficult decision to work for a private firm practicing tax law immediately upon graduating. Her original goal was to pay down her school loans but the salary she was making afforded her a really nice apartment in Chelsea that she shared with her law school roommate, and a lifestyle that she soon got used to. She found she was not paying any extra on her school loans. Maria began to discover, though, that her values were very different from her colleagues' values. She considers herself pretty moderate but was often teased at work by her co-workers for what they considered her "liberal" views. Slowly, she noticed that her core values were beginning to change and she could imagine herself in a house in the suburbs with all the materialistic trappings. This realization scared her and, coupled with a growing unhappiness at work, she decided to leave the practice after two years. "I felt that, in the end, I was just helping companies figure out how not to pay taxes . . . I felt like I was betraying what I wanted to do." She was miserable.

Since 1994, Maria has lived true to her values and her commitment to public interest law. To make the leap from the private firm to the public sector, she had to move back in with her parents in Washington Heights for about 18 months while she saved money to be able to afford living on her own at a public interest salary. She describes her first years at Legal Services as an incredible relief. Starting at about $32,000 a year, she practiced housing law in Brooklyn. Housing court was extremely stressful, "it was kind of a madhouse," and her colleagues would now tease her in a good-natured way for loving the work so much. She says, "I just loved it. I was back to being me."

Since 1998 Maria has practiced immigration law in a nonprofit organization where she defends people against deportation. NYU's LRAP paid approximately $1,200 a year for two years on her school loans once she started working at Legal Services. The LRAP payments ended along with her stay at her parents' house when she got married in 1994. Maria's husband is also a public interest lawyer.

A picture of their four-and-a-half-year-old daughter graces Maria's desk. The adorable little girl is at the forefront of Maria's financial concerns. Although she and her husband are both earning good salaries, it is substantially less than they would have made in private practice. To make ends meet, they reside in upper Manhattan, a considerable commute, creating long stretches away from their daughter. They were finally able to afford to buy an apartment after years of saving. Maria and her husband are used to sacrificing to do the work they love to do. Maria smiles as she recalls that many of her friends travel to Greece and other remote locations for vacations while she and her family go to the Jersey shore, but she is quick to add, "We're still pretty happy with our decision."

Maria worries about her daughter's schooling. She does not want her daughter attending the same type of "tough" schools she experienced growing up. They had hoped to send her to a public school on the Upper West Side but did not get lucky in the out-of-district lottery. After touring many private and public schools, comparing them, and weighing the harsh financial reality, Maria and Juan decided to send their daughter to private school at a considerable cost. It's not only the cost Maria thinks about, but also the impact on her daughter once she is aware of the differences between what her family can afford and the lifestyles her classmates enjoy. Despite these worries and financial realities, there's never been any real temptation to go back to the private sector.

Maria details a world of difference between her level of satisfaction with the work she does now as opposed to representing corporate clients:

> The people that I represent now are facing having to leave this country, for the most part, for relatively minor crimes that were committed many years ago. They're really treated like the lowest of the low. They're immigrants, they have convictions, they're poor and no one wants to hear about them. The immigration service can be a very nasty agency. I am fluent in Spanish, and I can help my clients through the process. So many clients tell me that just understanding the process, and being treated with respect is such a big deal for them. It's a lot of pressure for these families whose loved one is facing deportation, and when we win the cases, which fortunately we do a lot, it's very emotional. Everybody's crying and you feel that what you're doing is really rewarding.
>
> For example, I just represented a woman who the government wants to deport, who's bipolar. She has two disabled children, one who's deaf, and another son who has a depressive disorder. She had two theft offenses from many years ago. It basically sounds like her so-called friends were stealing in different apartments, and they left her as the scapegoat. She's been in this country legally for many years, since she was three or four years old and, if we lose, it will mean mandatory deportation. We were able to get the criminal case reopened in Georgia and there's a good argument for the other offense.
>
> And so it's just an amazing thing when somebody comes in and they're going to be mandatorily deported and now I think we are going to be

able to terminate the case. And it's for somebody who's been feeling very depressed and scared. She's so happy now. Those kinds of things are just, for me, really amazing, and really make the job worth it. At these times it feels really good to be able to get paid for what I really want to do.

D. A FULL HEART

Finally, someone who knows the challenges and rewards of public interest lawyering is Janine Hoft, who has practiced civil rights law (mostly for the People's Law Office in Chicago) since graduating law school. Janine's tireless and rigorous representation of people who otherwise would have no legal recourse is an inspiration to us all.

Janine Hoft

If there were a scale that measured passion about work, Janine (Jani) Hoft would break it. She's off-the-charts passionate about her work and the clients she represents at the People's Law Office in Chicago. Having practiced there since she graduated from Chicago-Kent College of Law in 1984, she is no less enthusiastic about lawyering for social change and racial justice than she was more than 20 years ago when she started. She says, "I can't imagine doing any other kind of law other than public interest law. There doesn't seem to me to be any point to doing anything else. I went to law school to do public interest law." Jani has mostly practiced civil rights law, with 99 percent of the cases she handles being cases involving police misconduct. The racism that permeates the police force that spreads throughout the criminal justice system is what Jani fights in civil courts on a daily basis. She describes it as follows:

> The idea has always been to us (at the People's Law
> Office), and the theory underlying Section 1983 work,

is that you hit the city and the corporation counsel in the pocketbook where they feel it and in that way force the city to make changes. They have to do their own cost benefit analysis and hopefully determine that brutal, insensitive, and obnoxious cops cost the city too much money. So they better make efforts to put a stop to brutality, ideally establishing better training programs and routing out those who are going to cause serious injury to predominantly black and Latino poor people in the city of Chicago.

These are related issues that I think need to come to light to promote social change. Racism is so connected in with police misconduct that it feels like both of those issues, in terms of government accountability and anti-racist work feel implicated by the work that we do.

The process of bringing civil police misconduct cases serves to change not only the dynamics of the police force, but also the judicial system, forcing judges and juries to actually see the people they so easily stereotype and dehumanize. Jani says:

That's what we do. We humanize a victim to the city and to the judge and if we get to a trial, to the jury. That's important to me in terms of social change, too. Making people outraged because I think police misconduct happens when we are silent. They are able to get away with it when people don't care or don't know about it.

Growing up with three older brothers, Jani credits her parents with teaching her about fairness and equality and modeling a commitment to social justice. Many people at the memorial service for her father in 2006 remembered him as a champion for the underdog. Jani says, "If he perceived you or someone he knew as an underdog he was very passionate about it. I really think he instilled that in me." On being the only daughter of four children, Jani reflects:

> My brothers, who were in my father's Boy Scout troop, felt like they were the dispossessed because he was very concerned about not being accused of nepotism so he was hardest on them. I look at my dad and even my standing in my family, being the only girl with three older brothers. I felt like people really did not take me seriously. I don't know if that perception was accurate but there was something about the power dynamic involving age and gender. My mom bent over backwards to treat all four of us equally; that is a strong value that came from my mother. She really stressed fairness and equality. I don't know how she did it. Even though we were three boys and a girl, we all got equal shares of everything. There were no bigger portions for the boys and all were expected to do the same chores.

In terms of social justice, Jani remembers one arena in which she felt somewhat misled by her parents. She says, "My parents brought me up thinking racism was bad but it was a thing of the past and things were a lot better now and there really wasn't anything to worry about." It wasn't until she took an urban studies program in college and spent a semester in Chicago that Jani realized how much racism and poverty there was in our society. Jani also took a course entitled Politics and Social Change at her undergraduate school, Macalester College in St. Paul, Minnesota, that introduced her to social justice theory. But nothing would prepare her for what she encountered in Chicago. It was a time when Harold Washington, an African-American candidate, was running for mayor of Chicago. Jani remembers "wearing a Washington campaign button and having a cab driver yell at me out the window that I was an 'N lover' just for wearing the button." It was during this life-changing semester, interning at a community law office in a

Puerto Rican neighborhood, that Jani decided to attend law school:

> During the urban studies program there were a lot of very moving experiences that I had around race and realizing that things were bad and there was a lot of social justice work that needed to happen. People told me that you should go to law school and I was really turned on by Chicago and the idea that you can't forget the social problems living here because they smack you in the face all the time. I decided that if I was going to practice law I wanted to practice in Chicago.

The progressive lawyers that Jani knew advised her to attend Chicago-Kent for law school. When she began law school, she questioned that advice thinking, "I walked into school the first day and I said, 'Why did they tell me to go here?' It was incredibly nondiverse. There were no Latinos at all in my entering class. There were no black men. There was one guy from Spain and there were two African-American women." Jani befriended the two African-American women, one of whom remarked when she was approached by Jani that she had waited weeks for a fellow law student to speak to her. She found out that she had attended the same urban studies program that Jani had been in during college. Ever the rebel, Jani was the first student in her class to challenge the Socratic method by admitting she wasn't prepared when called on by a professor. The class was aghast and Jani projects that they thought she had narrowly missed being struck by a lightning bolt.

The wisdom of the advice to attend Chicago-Kent Law School became clear to Jani when she enrolled in the criminal law clinic and got to know the clinic professors. Even though the professors didn't allow the students a lot of responsibility for the cases, she was glad to be exposed to good lawyers and get to see lawyering for social change in action. Jani found her best outlet for her desire to learn progressive lawyering to be working for a woman lawyer she had met during her internship at the community law office in college. The lawyer, Mara, ended up sharing office space in the People's Law Office and Jani became connected with the law office to which she would devote her legal career. But first Jani would graduate from law school and go on a solo bicycle trip.

When Jani started at the People's Law Office as an attorney, the salary negotiations took the form of the partners asking her how much money she needed to live on a monthly basis. Because Jani was living in an apartment with other people, didn't have a car, and was used to a spartan lifestyle from law school, she told them she would need $500 a month, quite a conservative figure, especially taking into account that she had borrowed $20,000 for law school, not having any independent sources of financial assistance. In the early 1980s, $20,000 of school loans was a considerable amount. Of the $500 a month she was being paid as a lawyer, $150 a month was going toward repayment of her school loans. Jani remembers, "It felt like a big paycheck compared with my income while a student when I couldn't work full time. I remember the first major purchase I made was a moped. I paid $200 for it when I got my first lawyer paycheck so I could buzz around on that."

Within six months, Jani was made a partner at the firm and received what she considered a "huge raise" to $800 a month. In 1984, Jani was earning less than $10,000 a year. In addition, the partners made it clear to her that, during lean times for the firm, the staff would get paid first before the partners so the possibility of missing a paycheck was ever present. Jani realized she needed to be prepared to live on very little. Still, Jani viewed herself as fortunate:

> I think I actually missed a paycheck only one or two times. It never really became a huge issue for me in terms of the salary. Granted, I'm a minimalist and the other partners were older and starting to get into different situations by the time I came into the People's Law Office. They all used to live in the same apartment together. I'm glad I missed those days.

The attorneys started having families, moving, and thinking of retirement funds. Salaries and fairness became a constant conversation and mostly led to a climate where raises were based on need. As a single woman without children, Jani got paid less than others with families. Being the minimalist she is, Jani did fine in a co-op apartment with very low rent and an old car, but explains:

> For the last, at least half of the time I've been at the People's Law Office, I've *needed* to go on a vacation to the Caribbean once a year. I used to not do that. As you get older your minimalism expands and the office was able to accommodate that, too. They were able to accommodate people having kids, buying houses, taking vacations, living alone, not having to share living spaces.

The firm has infrequently detoured into taking other than civil rights cases, thinking that real estate closings or divorce work might provide more of a steady income as bread-and-butter cases. But they've never traveled that path for very long and have always handled predominantly civil rights cases. Presently, their caseload is only civil rights cases. Jani was on "sabbatical" from the firm for three years when she taught the public interest law clinic at Syracuse University College of Law in the mid-1990s and, when she returned, the partners discouraged her from taking divorces although it made sense to her feminist theory of the practice of law. At times, when money was tight at the firm and attorneys would leave, the partners would devise a severance package favoring attorneys who continued in public interest law jobs.

Jani's advice to law students wanting to pursue public interest work is simple: "Stay true to your ideals." She adds:

> I can't imagine what kind of person I would be or how I would feel about myself if I hadn't continued in public interest law. Just talk about the possibilities, when you think about how people get jobs and it

> really is often a crapshoot. I almost didn't ask to work here because I assumed they would not have the money to hire me. But particularly when they found out how little I needed to make, we worked it out.

Jani's passion for working for the betterment of society, determination to help people less fortunate, and other-than-financial motivation landed her where she is. If the work at the People's Law Office had not materialized, Jani would have found a way to pursue her passion for public interest law in some way or another. The world's a better place for having Jani Hoft in it.

E. CONCLUSION

Public interest lawyers show up at work each morning with their minds, hearts, and souls. The rewards for integrating the whole self into work are vast and enormous. They are rewards that money cannot buy. Of course there are struggles, challenges, and difficulties. It's not easy work. Hard work with only monetary reward quickly becomes unsustainable and shallow. Being motivated by money will never bring about passion for work. But hard work fueled by passion and commitment to helping others is sustainable beyond the monetary hardships. And, as we've seen, greater happiness and job satisfaction are attainable by following one's heart and passion. As it turns out the old adage is true: Money cannot buy happiness. Passion at work brings happiness.

CHAPTER 6

The Journey Revisited

There's one other piece of sage advice that has always stayed
with me and guided me in this journey called life (in addition to
"Don't let the money stop you"). When I was 17 years old and
graduating from high school, we had a family friend, Jack, who
was probably in his late 40s. He was dying of cancer. I remember
he took the time to write me a card for graduation. Although I
haven't found the card since about two moves ago, I'll never forget
the last line: "Never compromise yourself." At the time, I wasn't
capable of understanding the true impact of those words he wrote.
Neither did I understand how hard they are to live by. I didn't realize
how many opportunities and temptations there are in life to do just
that, to compromise yourself. It would take many years for me to
have a strong enough concept of whom this "self" really is to know

what it is that I wasn't supposed to compromise. The implications of Jack's advice are incredibly far-reaching. As I look back on the 35 or so years since reading those words in his card, I consider myself extremely fortunate that I had those words reverberating in my head as I pondered many of life's choices.

Sometimes it's really hard advice to live by, as we feel, think, and grope our way through choices in life. I almost quit law school after my first year. I was miserable. The Socratic method of teaching, the quantity of appellate case upon appellate case to be read, briefed, digested, analyzed, and regurgitated left me drained and lifeless. The creative juices that had been flowing freely in college, the mind expansion that was stimulated by studying global issues and cosmic concerns, with the exploration of deep "why are we here" questions were cut off at the source. They were replaced with more casebook reading than physically possible, cases filled with one-dimensional people in an adversarial judicial system that brought out the worst in everyone. Add to that the most intimidating learning environment I had experienced in my life. On top of everything, one of my house-mates was diagnosed with Hodgkin's disease (cancer in the lymph glands) during my second semester, and I was in and out of the hospital visiting her, taking her for radiation treatments, and staying up nights as she wondered whether she would live or die. When I asked the powers that be in the law school for a little slack on the final exam schedule (final exams were the one and only grade determiner), I was met with a cold-hearted, unrelenting "No."

I was miserable. If not for not-so-subtle parental persuasion and having already invested thousands of dollars, real and borrowed, I would have walked away, to what I do not know. I was raised with the "we finish what we start" principle; "don't be a quitter" was engrained in me from an early age. I also thought, "What's another two years in the scheme of things?" Better to tough it out than throw away a whole year, with nothing to show for it but the loan payments. I found out soon enough, when I started my second year of law school, that I was, in fact, not compromising myself, and had made the right decision in returning to law school. Having received a work-study stipend, I got a job as a law clerk at the Legal Aid Bureau of Buffalo. It gave life to the experience of studying law for me and provided my life at the time with meaning. I loved it. I was no longer miserable. I was helping people.

In hindsight, I have no regrets. My law degree has given me the opportunity to be of service in this world in a way that I could never have imagined; developing skills to provide others with opportunities to improve their own lives and communities; and teaching others to do the same. My point is simple: To not compromise in a world that asks you to compromise your values and principles at every turn can be extremely challenging. Rising to that challenge is equally rewarding; the greater the challenge, the greater the reward, in my humble experience.

A huge part of not compromising yourself is following your heart, respecting the call to dedicate yourself to what you are passionate about, and believing in yourself enough to listen to the innermost voices guiding you. Staying true to your deepest beliefs and values is often a scary process in our world today. There is so much pressure to conform. I daresay law school is one of the worst offenders and it will take Herculean efforts to follow your own path when that path takes you through a legal education. Especially for those following their hearts to a career in public interest law, law school is not a supportive environment. The world is a scary place even for those most intent on conformity. It's so ironic that the legal profession, an institution with the power to bring about the greatest nonviolent change in the world, so strives for conformity and maintenance of the status quo. If you are called to challenge that status quo, if changing the world for the better is why you pursue a law degree, please, please keep your eye on the prize. As the public interest lawyers whose lives illuminate the pages of this book show, the legal profession can stretch and grow and change for the better. Justice and fairness for all can be the goal of good lawyering, not just the transference of wealth from one corporation or wealthy entity to another. Going against the tide requires strength, endurance, and commitment, but nothing is ever achieved without struggle and perseverance.

Passion also demands risk. It's a risky business following one's passion, but playing it safe in life resigns one to complacency.

The good news is that there are ways to lessen the risk. One way is to trust yourself, trust that inner voice, and trust the voice of your heart to guide you well. Don't be afraid to rely on knowledge that comes from places in addition to your analytical mind, such as your heart, your gut, perhaps even your subconscious. There are ways to access the full range of information available to us. Learn how to meditate. Really. It's a great stress reducer in addition to helping quiet the analytical mind so that other sources of wisdom from within can be heard. Sit or walk quietly and alone in nature. Don't question the thoughts and insights that might arise from the silence. Who knows, you might even be fortunate enough to be given advice by a tree, a chipmunk, a flower, or a hawk. Just absorb it and sit with it. You're alone, remember? No one can question your sanity! You might also want to learn how to work with your dreams to see what messages your subconscious might have hidden for you there.

The point is to explore whatever avenues of knowing there are in this mysterious existence and to trust the messages you receive. The endless string of thoughts that make up the analytical mind are just a fraction of the wisdom that's available from within us. If you're still with me, as long as we're pushing the edge, I may be so bold as to suggest that you pray for guidance. Even if you don't believe in God, pray to the unknown, pray to whatever source there is in yourself that guides you throughout the day. My experience has been that when I'm not praying for a specific outcome, but instead when I pray for guidance and strength and love, my prayers are answered. I receive the guidance I need. It doesn't even matter that I don't know where the answer is coming from. That's what trust is all about. It's not about blind faith but trust in myself, trust in my instincts, and trust in the unknown forces guiding me.

———————————————

It's been my experience, in my 53 years of life, that when I am doing work out of passion and love of the work, the universe finds ways to support me. My first job out of law school paid $14,000 a year, which, even in 1980, was barely enough to live on. I took the job because I was passionate about working in the environmental law field and I wanted to work for the not-for-profit environmental organization that offered me a job no matter how low the pay. My very first case out of law school involved challenging the U.S. Department of Commerce's decision to issue permits to the Japanese Salmon Fisheries Association to kill marine mammals, including porpoises, whales, and sea lions, in their fishing operations. I was in U.S. District Court in the District of Columbia arguing procedural questions of administrative law against seasoned government lawyers and one of the best law firms in DC hired by the government of Japan. In ruling that the Department of Commerce had not acted contrary to the substantial weight of the evidence, the judge stated in open court and in his written opinion that, if he was deciding the case *de novo,* he would have ruled in our favor and against the government. But, due to the standard of administrative review he was obliged to follow, he had no choice. I didn't win the case or save the porpoises, but I gave it my all, giving voice to the voiceless, fighting for the defenseless. Soon thereafter, within the first six months working at the environmental organization, my salary increased from $14,000 to $20,000 a year (still hardly enough to live on in the metropolitan New York City area . . . but, a gold mine for me at the time). The lawsuit was successful in being part of mounting legal and political pressure on the Japanese government and their fishing operations to eliminate the killing of marine mammals in the industry.

I have continued pursuing work I love and feel good about doing, from environmental law to poverty law to not-for-profit organizations law to community development law, for the almost 30 years of my legal career. I am now earning several times over the $20,000 a year I was earning in 1982, an incredible salary for someone who has committed herself to public interest law her whole life. My point, and the point of the story, is that if you follow your passion, the universe will support you, financially and otherwise. Or, in the reverse, it's been said, "If you fall into the trap of measuring your worth by money, you will always feel inadequate. . . . Thus, when, as is true in law firms, more money almost always means more work, money not only fails to buy happiness, but it actually buys unhappiness."[44]

Moving to Syracuse, New York, in 1984, I knew I would continue in public interest law. It would be eight months before an attorney position opened at Legal Services of Central New York, which I applied for and was offered. I started at Legal Services at an annual salary in the high $20,000 range, about $28,000 if memory serves me. The specialty law unit I would soon be incorporated into was the Housing Unit. We mostly did eviction defense, with an occasional affirmative lawsuit against a particularly egregious landlord. The plight of poor people desperately trying to hold onto substandard apartments was heartbreaking for me. The receptionist at Legal Services put it in perspective one day as I came back to the office from court, somewhat gleeful that I had won an eviction defense proceeding where nonpayment of rent was the issue. Upon my proclamation, "We won, we won," Ray, the receptionist said, "Oh, you got them another month in the apartment?" Ray was cognizant of the fact that a private landlord can give a month's notice to vacate at any time to a month-to-month tenant, even if the rent is paid in full. My ego deflated, as the realization was overwhelming that I was providing only very temporary relief to a family caught in the vicious cycle of poverty.

After a year of defending evictions, the universe heard my cry. At the Legal Services office where I worked, the attorneys would rotate intake and I happened to be the attorney assigned to intake appointments the day a husband and wife came into the office and wrote in the small box on the intake sheet provided to "describe your problem" that "We want to buy our house in tax foreclosure from our landlord." This family of seven (five children, including a set of twins) had been renting a substandard single-family house from a landlord who took their rent money every month and did nothing to improve the condition of the house. He had not been putting any money back into the house, even to pay the real property taxes.

---

44. Patrick J. Schiltz, "Attorney Well-Being in Large Firms: Choices Facing Young Lawyers," 52 *Vanderbilt Law Review* 871 (May 1999): 921-922.

The couple had called the City Assessor's office and had found out that the landlord was so delinquent in the property taxes that the city could take the property from him involuntarily in a tax foreclosure sale and sell it to them for the assessed value, which was incredibly low, due to the condition of the house. In case you're wondering, this was not a typical Legal Services case at the time. It was a one in a million chance to be on intake when such a unique client and case came in the door of the office. It was fate (or circumstance, depending on your belief system). I not only represented the family in buying the house out from under the landlord in the tax foreclosure proceeding, but I also was able to access state funds from the New York State Housing Trust Fund program, which was in its infancy in 1985. We received $50,000 for the family to rehabilitate the house and make it livable. It was like *Extreme Makeover: Home Edition* before TV producers ever got the idea. One of my most memorable moments as an attorney came at the end of this process when the family came in to sign some final documents and the parents brought all five children into the office. One of the five-year-old twins asked, "Mommy, are they going to get us new furniture?" My fate was sealed. They would be in the house for much longer than 30 days, ever free from the threat of eviction. I had helped a low-income family improve their living situation far beyond their wildest dreams. They were owners of a house they were proud to call home.

From there, the opportunities along my path abounded. I represented tenant's associations buying their multifamily apartment buildings from their landlords in much the same way as the single family had done. I helped low-income renters convert their buildings to not-for-profit cooperative housing, the goal being for each of the tenants to have an interest in their housing. I researched the concept of community land trusts, just becoming known in the late 1980s, as a vehicle to provide quality, affordable housing to low-income people, and ended up representing community organizations involved in improving low-income neighborhoods and the lives of the people who resided in the neighborhoods. I was very fortunate that the executive director of Legal Services at the time was very supportive of groundbreaking approaches to assisting people living in poverty.

One of my favorite aspects of the job at that point, which has remained one of my favorite parts, was walking down the street of a deteriorated neighborhood, entering a dilapidated old building, imagining its transformation, and then witnessing and being a part of building after building in the neighborhood being gutted and rehabilitated into quality, comfortable housing for a family or individual who had only known substandard housing.

The universe continued to support me and the work I loved when, in the summer of 1989, I was approached by faculty at the College of Law at Syracuse University and asked to apply for a position in the newly formed Housing and Finance Clinic. Two professors at the law school had found funding to start a transactional clinic that would practice affordable housing development law. I applied for the position and the rest, as they say, is herstory.

So, what is my advice to you? I have been blessed with good advice in my life. I would like to pass it along with some of my own. There are two pieces of advice I'd like to convey and, in contrast to the two pieces I passed along from others that contained negations — "Don't let the money stop you" and "Never compromise yourself" — I would like to phrase my advice in the positive.

The first morsel of wisdom actually comes from a refrigerator magnet. I don't usually quote my refrigerator magnets, let alone remember where I get them and in what year, but I'll never forget that in March 1999, my friend Leslie Bender gave me a refrigerator magnet that said "If you're not living on the edge, you're taking up too much space." Putting a positive twist on it, I'd say, "Live on the edge." It's the place where you can find your best balance. It's also a place of incredible scenery in all directions. Living on the edge, being true to your values, following your heart, living your passion, can be exciting and rewarding. But, it is very scary at times. You'll be on the fringes of the legal system if you're committed to public interest law. You'll be out on the edge, looking down into the chasm. But you'll also find room to stretch and grow in ways you never would have gotten the chance to if you backed away from the edge. You'll be surrounded by breathtaking views that you couldn't even imagine a few yards back from the edge.

Leslie gave me that refrigerator magnet at a time in my life when I was closest to the edge. In 1999, I decided to take my commitment to public interest and civil rights to the next level. I was about to leave on a human rights delegation to Chiapas, Mexico. The state of Chiapas in Mexico had been in a state of unrest and military repression since January 1, 1994, when the Zapatistas, a revolutionary movement of indigenous peoples in Mexico, momentarily seized power after an armed conflict in Chiapas. The Zapatistas continue to insist on basic human rights for indigenous people in Mexico as they did from the beginning of their revolution. Their 11 demands include work, land, shelter, food, health, education, independence, freedom, democracy, justice, and peace. To have their demands heard they staged the rebellion on the day that the North American Free Trade Agreement (NAFTA) was implemented. NAFTA has far-reaching impacts for the indigenous people of Mexico, furthering the polarization of wealth and increasing the effects of poverty on the already poor, native people in Mexico. The effect of NAFTA is to put the 11 simple demands of the indigenous people even further out of their reach.

The Mexican army quickly moved in to quell the rebellion and militarized the state of Chiapas. The Zapatistas dispersed to remote locations and indigenous peoples' lives worsened under the constant intimidation and surveillance of the army. I remember reading about the Zapatista rebellion in the newspapers. It made national headlines for a short time as the New Year's Day rebellion. It captured my attention, their struggle captured my heart, and, although I consider myself a pacifist, never condoning violence, the plight of a people oppressed for more than 500 years in their native land lit up my soul. I followed their story and struggles, their shouts for basic human rights, for the years following until December 22, 1997, when the paramilitary forces that were supported by the government perpetrated a brutal massacre in the village of Acteal in Chiapas. For years, the paramilitary units had been kidnapping, torturing, and killing indigenous people throughout Chiapas in villages where there were suspected Zapatista sympathizers, but this was by far the worst massacre. Forty-five members of the pacifist arm of the Zapatista movement, Las Abejas (the Bees) were gunned down during a prayer service in the village church. The massacre took several hours, during which time soldiers at a local government army base did absolutely nothing despite knowing that the massacre was occurring. Of the 45 people slain, 15 were children, 21 were women (4 of whom were pregnant), and 9 were men. When I heard during the spring of 1998 that there would be a Witness for Peace human rights delegation traveling to Chiapas and spending time in Acteal, I signed on to go. I was definitely living on my edge.

As we stood in the church where the massacre had taken place, silently observing the memorial to the men, women, and children who had been killed, one of the women in our delegation began sobbing. Our guide, a Mayan man, began comforting her. This man had lived in Acteal for years, had witnessed the massacre, had helped bury the dead, some of whom were his relatives, had helped build the memorial, and *he* was comforting *her*. This man who had seen so much suffering and misery, who lived in a place without the most basic comforts that we Americans take for granted, reached out to comfort a stranger from a country whose policies help cause the suffering and misery of his people. Another lesson in living on the edge: If you're scared you're going to fall, get outside yourself, stop thinking about yourself on the edge, and reach out to someone else.

My last piece of advice is the hardest to follow. Be authentic. In this life, especially in the United States, there are many invitations to be inauthentic. I invite you to be authentic. To be authentic you have to find and follow your own truth. The best place to find your truth is in your heart. It's not in your logical mind; it's in your heart. In fact, to hear what's in your heart, you have to quiet your mind. The nonstop chatter of your mind confuses the truth. As I once heard on a tape about meditation, how can you trust your mind?[45] Your mind is the thing that tells you, "Go ahead, eat that piece of chocolate cake, ooh, it looks so good, it'll taste great, go ahead, eat it." Then, 30 seconds after you've eaten the piece of chocolate cake, your mind says, "Why the heck did you eat that piece of cake, you fat pig? You know how many calories were in that one piece of cake you just ate? You're going to have to go to the gym for an hour just to work off that one piece of chocolate cake."

Authenticity is not the forté of the ego. Your ego wants you to fit in at all costs, even if it means being inauthentic. Your ego will be chattering away about the risks of being truly authentic. It will use humiliation, criticism, and judgment to try to talk you into conforming to perceived norms. Do not trust your ego. Fortunately, you can help your ego let go of the need to follow perceived external dictates by listening deep down to your heart and the yearnings deep down at your center. Your heart and soul are your guides to authenticity and fulfillment of your true purpose in life. Listen deeply to find what truly motivates you and brings you joy. You can only find joy in life if you're living your values and being true to your core. Be authentic. In the transitional, life-changing decisions and in the seemingly unimportant day-to-day decisions, be authentic. Each one of us has something unique to offer this world. Keep searching until you discover what it is. Tirelessly pursue bringing your uniqueness to the world. Be authentic. You'll be surprised at how the universe supports you. The universe loves authenticity.

---

45. I believe the tape was narrated by Joseph and Andrea Levine, from a workshop on meditation they gave.

CHAPTER 7

Afterword

Originally, my goal in writing this book was to inspire law students to maintain their commitment to public interest law. I hope I've achieved that purpose. The process of researching the book, interviewing the lawyers, and writing the book has been a transformative experience for me. During this process, I've been living the struggles, challenges, and rewards I encourage others to face and persevere through in these pages. I've struggled with doubt and insecurity about the value of what I'm writing. I've dealt with challenges in the writing I never dreamed I'd have to face. Writing this book has been my own lesson in risk taking, in keeping my heart open, and in being authentic. I have had to take my own advice, following my passion, finding my authenticity, and grounding myself in the challenge of the process, allowing the outcome to unfold of its own accord. It's been a journey of faith, believing that the greatest gifts come through climbing over the biggest obstacles. The challenge is always to be able to hold that belief during the climb, not being able to see what's on the other side. My evolving goal in writing this book has been to convey this truth that is in my heart.

At the beginning of my second year of law school, a five-week-old orphaned, stray kitten found me and convinced me to take him home with me. I had always fancied myself a dog person, distanced by the aloofness of cats and their apparent elite attitude. The cat I would come to call Candide, as he really did have the best of all possible worlds,[46] won my heart from the moment I laid eyes on him. He was a bundle of purring orange fur who wanted little more in life than a scratch behind the ears, an endless belly rub, and treats after dinner. Because I did most of my studying at home during law school, Candide and I spent a lot of time together those first couple of years. I began to refer to him, not so jokingly, as the man of my dreams.

I had 14 wonderful years of living with Candide. We moved together more times than I remember (at least eight). He was my confessor, confidante, and the one constant through the joys of new relationships and the sorrows of failed relationships, the transitions to new jobs, and the ups and downs of life and love so intensified and relentless in one's twenties. On April 10, 1992, when Candide took his last breath and purred his last purr on this earthly realm, it felt like a huge part of me had been ripped out from somewhere deep inside. Although I had been through the death of my beloved grandfather when I was 19 years old and I had grieved the loss of my childhood dog, Gretal, I had never seen a dead body. When I came home the day Candide died and found his sweet furry body on the bed, I had no idea what lessons in death and dying were in store

---

46. *Candide* is a book written by Voltaire in the eighteenth century.

for me. It would take me many years to find the priceless gifts in those lessons.

Four months after saying goodbye to Candide, my father, my one source of unconditional love in life other than my animals, died very suddenly and unexpectedly. It was August 23, 1992. My grief was truly boundless, to become amorphously surreal and multidimensional four months later when my mother became ill with the cancer that would ultimately cause her death two years after my father's on July 8, 1994. The man I was living with, Paul, and I were the primary caregivers for my mom during her dying as we were with his mom who died on September 1, 1993, after a long struggle with breast cancer. When Paul and I met in the fall of 1991, we had three living parents between us. Within three years, we had none.

During those years I was also in the crucial years of my tenure track as a law professor. Caring for my mother was my priority and I struggled with the meaning of writing law review articles while literally dealing with life and death every waking and some sleeping moments. Somehow I persevered. I look back at that time and I honestly don't know how I got through. Something beyond my knowing was definitely guiding me. There was a glimmer of that guidance almost a year after my father died when I saw a notice in the paper about a one-day women's meditation retreat at the Zen Center of Syracuse. I had been pondering how to mark the anniversary of my father's passing and, as it turned out, the retreat was to be held on August 23, 1993, the one-year anniversary. It would be the beginning of my continued dedication to a meditation practice that has helped keep me centered and aware through the best and worst of times.

The gifts of the heart-breaking, gut-wrenching, mind-numbing years of the dying, death, and mourning of my parents would slowly unfold. My journey through the doorway of heart to soul was facilitated by the trauma of those years. My parents left me with a legacy of love and grace that has endured, grown, and blossomed over the years since their physical lives came to an end.

In 1996 I received tenure at the law school and in 1999-2000 I took my first sabbatical. I was able to take a year-long leave from teaching due to a small inheritance from my parents, who had been saving for a retirement together they never got to experience. Having lived frugally all their lives, never making much money, and saving what little they could, my parents died full of dreams for their retirement and bank accounts my sister and I did not even know existed. Of course, I determined not to make the same mistake and took advantage of the chance to explore my inner and outer worlds before it was too late. Drawn to a small announcement in the back of the Omega Institute catalog for a "visionquest" in the canyonlands of Utah, I embarked on what would be the first of two solo wilderness journeys, supported by guides and experts in the physical, emotional, and spiritual preparation for descent to the soul. Among the many teachings and gifts of my two visionquests (the second would be two years later) was the discovery of my inner core, underneath the layers of fear, societal expectation, ego, and insecurity. I was to uncover a deep sense of my own power, an inner power (not power over others) that could be accessed and drawn on when needed; a power from within yet connected to a source far greater than any one person. The journey of loss, grief, exploration, and healing I had been on since the death of Candide became bountiful in its gifts.

The struggles of life, love, money, and work easily overshadow that deep sense of knowing and connection. As the daily routines and surprises conspire to distance us from ourselves, we need to find daily rituals to nurture that which is best within us. For lawyers there can be a great disconnect, called on from early in our schooling, to favor logic and our analytical minds to solve problems. Writing this book, meeting the lawyers I interviewed, privileged to have a glimpse into their hearts and souls, I am reminded of the extreme importance of giving equal voice to our hearts and our souls. There is so much to be learned when we quiet the analytical mind. Find work you love to do and you'll be on the road to happiness and fulfillment. Our working lives take too much of our time to be pursued only for a paycheck. Pursue your passions.

Perhaps that journey through an open heart to soul will find us on a path we would have never imagined, a path away from societal expectations and motivation of the almighty dollar. Looking around at the scenery, it might be different than what you expected. Enjoy the view. Take deep breaths and find courage from within. Not only is it okay to take your own path, not following the crowd, but there is great reward in it.

The United States is considered the "richest" nation in the world. Just imagine if what was referred to in that sentiment was the richness of our hearts and our soulfulness; if our country was known for its big heart. Imagine if we acknowledged our interconnectedness and acted on the knowledge that we're all in this life together, if we were motivated primarily by love, not money. Let's start with the lawyers.

Loan Repayment Assistance Programs

State LRAPs: Programs and Eligibility*

STATE	PROGRAM NAME	PROGRAM DESCRIPTION
Alabama	None	
Alaska	None	
Arizona	Arizona Foundation for Legal Services & Education Loan Repayment Program	The AFLSELRP is a statewide program that assists attorneys employed in nonprofit organizations who are dedicated to serving the legal needs of low-income individuals and families in Arizona.
Arkansas	None	
California	Program not funded	In the fall of 2001, California Governor Gray Davis signed AB 935, which authorized the creation of a loan repayment program for legal aid attorneys, prosecutors, public defenders, and county attorneys who handle child support cases. There is no funding for this bill. If and when the program is funded, it will be administered by a state agency. To access a copy of the bill, visit http://www.assembly.ca.gov/acs/defaulttext.asp (search for AB 935).
Colorado	None	
Connecticut	None	
Delaware	None	
District of Columbia	Foundation LRAP DC Poverty LRAP	These LRAPs are for lawyers employed in Washington, DC in nonprofit organizations serving the legal needs of low-income or underrepresented individuals.
Florida	Florida Bar Foundation's Loan Repayment Assistance Program	Program not currently funded.
Georgia	State program created but not funded	
Hawaii	None	
Idaho	None	

*Current as of December 2008

180

ELIGIBILITY		
LICENSURE & EMPLOYMENT REQUIREMENTS	**INCOME**	**ELIGIBLE LOANS**
Applicants must be members of the Arizona Bar and be employed by an approved nonprofit legal organization.	Income may not exceed $65,000.	Undergraduate and law school loans are determined for assistance.
Applicants must have graduated from an ABA accredited law school, be licensed to practice in DC or pending admission to practice, have full- or part-time employment with a nonprofit organization in DC that provides legal services to poor and underserved, and be a resident of DC (only for DC Poverty Lawyer LRAP).	Income may not exceed $65,000	Foundation LRAP participants receive help with both undergraduate and other graduate school loans, whereas the DC Poverty Lawyer LRAP only helps with law school debt.

continued on page 182

STATE	PROGRAM NAME	PROGRAM DESCRIPTION
Illinois	Loan Forgiveness Program	SB 1923, introduced in January 2008, would provide loan repayment assistance through the Illinois Student Assistance Commission to assistant state attorneys, assistant public defenders, civil legal aid attorneys, assistant attorneys general, and assistant public guardians. The bill had not passed as of November 2008.
Indiana	Indiana Bar Foundation Loan Repayment Assistance Program (LRAP-IN)	LRAP-IN gives assistance to applicants who would otherwise be precluded from working in qualifying employment because the salaries of civil legal aid organizations often do not support applicants' student loan debt.
Iowa	Iowa State Bar Association Loan Repayment Assistance Program (ISBA-LRAP)	The LRAP is designed to help law school graduates choose and maintain public interest employment by providing assistance to participants in repaying their student loans.
Kansas	None	
Kentucky	Public Service Student Law School Loan Assistance Program	Introduced in February 2004, HB 483 would have created the Public Service Student Law School Loan Assistance Program to reimburse full- or part-time prosecutors (attorney generals, commonwealth attorneys, county attorneys), public advocates, and legal services lawyers for payment of student law school loan expenses. The program would be funded by 2% of Kentucky's Court Cost Distribution Fund up to $1.2 million. The bill had not passed as of November 2008.
Louisiana	Public Interest Attorney Loan Repayment Assistance Program	In an effort to improve the recruitment and retention of highly qualified attorneys at Louisiana's civil legal aid providers, the Bar Foundation created its LRAP. The program offers financial assistance to public interest attorneys carrying law school debt.
Maine	Maine Bar Foundation Loan Repayment Assistance Program	The Maine Bar Foundation supports a loan program to assist attorneys interested in public service with repayment of their law school debts. Attorneys must be employed by participating legal service providers.

ELIGIBILITY		
LICENSURE & EMPLOYMENT REQUIREMENTS	**INCOME**	**ELIGIBLE LOANS**
Participants must be licensed to practice law in Indiana, be active members of the Indiana state bar association, and must be employed by a qualifying civil legal aid employer.	Income may not exceed $50,000.	Undergraduate, graduate, and law school loans.
Applicants must be licensed to practice law in Iowa (applicants may apply while waiting to take the bar exam or while awaiting admission, but will not receive assistance until admitted), be employed full time by October 1 at a qualifying public interest organiztion, and be active members of the Iowa State Bar Association.	Income may not exceed $50,000.	Undergraduate, graduate, and law school loans.
Applicants must be members of the Louisiana State Bar Association and be employed full-time by a nonprofit legal organization assisting low-income individuals that is financially supported by the Louisiana Bar Foundation.	The individual applicant's qualifying gross annual income may not exceed $45,000. There is also a married status income cap of $100,000 combined gross annual income. Applicants may adjust their income downward $5,000 per dependent.	Only applies to law school debt, undergraduate debt not counted.
All attorneys employed by nonprofit organizations in Maine whose primary purpose is to provide legal aid to the poor and/or disadvantaged are eligible.	The formula and extent of assistance are subject to change annually, depending on the availability of funds and the aggregate extent of need shown on the annual applications. Only applicant's income is taken into account.	Only applies to law school debt, undergraduate debt not counted.

continued on page 184

STATE	PROGRAM NAME	PROGRAM DESCRIPTION
Maryland	Janet L. Hoffman Loan Assistance Repayment Program	Maryland residents who provide public service in Maryland state or local government or nonprofit agencies in Maryland to low-income or underserved residents may apply for the program.
Massachusetts	Legislation introduced in 2005.	Massachusetts has not yet enacted legislation to create this LRAP. In 2005, Representative Eugene O'Flaherty of Chelsea introduced House Bill 01772, a petition "to establish a program to provide assistance with the repayment of educational loans associated with obtaining a law degree to law school graduates who are employed full-time in public service and who have income below specified levels." The bill had not passed as of November 2008.
Michigan	Program vetoed	In 2002, Michigan Goevernor Engler vetoed the section of HB 5648 that provided funding for a debt management loan program for attorneys employed by legal services organizations.
Minnesota	Loan Repayment Assistance Program of Minnesota	LRAP is a nonprofit organization with a mission to ensure that low-income and disadvantaged populations have access to competent counsel. LRAP works to achieve this mission by helping new attorneys who would like to enter public interest law scale the barrier posed by high education debt and low salaries.
Mississippi	None	
Missouri	Missouri Bar Loan Repayment Assistance Program	Although a wide range of positions qualify for awards, until funding is expanded, priority will be given to attorneys working for the Missouri State Public Defender System, criminal prosecutors, and legal services attorneys.

ELIGIBILITY		
LICENSURE & EMPLOYMENT REQUIREMENTS	**INCOME**	**ELIGIBLE LOANS**
Applicants must have graduated from a Maryland law school, be a full-time employee of a state or local government or in a nonprofit organization in Maryland. Employer must help low-income or underserved residents of areas of the state. Third-year law students attending a Maryland law school must submit a Pre-Graduation Law Application before graduation in May, together with verification of an employment offer. Law students must also submit a LARP general application.	If married, your individual annual gross salary cannot exceed $60,000, and your combined salaries cannot exceed $130,000.	Only educational loans from a university, government, or commercial source used to pay for education may be forgiven.
Applicants must be a graduate of a Minnesota law school working full-time in qualifying employment, or be a graduate of an ABA accredited law school working full-time in qualifying employment in Minnesota. Applicants who have never received an LRAP award must be within three years of graduation.	Adjusted income (see special guidelines) must fall below $47,500.	Undergraduate, graduate, and joint degree loans from an institutional source qualify.
An applicant must have earned a JD from an ABA approved law school within the last three years; have been admitted to the Missouri Bar; and be a member in good standing. An applicant must be employed to work at least 35 hours per week in the state of Missouri in a law-related position for a nonprofit whose primary function is to provide legal advice or representation based on financial eligibility criteria, local, state, or federal government and certain positions within court systems.	An applicant must have an adjusted gross income for the Missouri Bar LRAP purposes at or below $45,999.	Debt must have been incurred through institutional sources to pursue law school or joint legal and graduate school degrees.

continued on page 186

STATE	PROGRAM NAME	PROGRAM DESCRIPTION
Montana	Montana Justice Foundation Loan Repayment Program	The Foundation's LRAP was established in January 2006 as a statewide LRAP for law school graduates employed in nonprofit organizations dedicated to serving the legal needs of low-income individuals and families in Montana.
Nebraska	Program pending	In 2007 Nelnet, as part of an agreement with Nebraska's Attorney General Jon Bruning, agreed to pay $500,000 into a trust fund established on behalf of Legal Aid of Nebraska at the Omaha Community Foundation. The interest from the trust will fund an LRAP.
Nevada	None	
New Hampshire	New Hampshire Bar Foundation Loan Forgiveness Assistance Program	The Law School LRAP provides law school loan assistance, in the form of forgivable loans, to ensure the ability of New Hampshire Legal Assistance, Legal Advice and Referral Center, Disabilities Rights Center, and New Hampshire Pro Bono to recruit and maintain a diverse body of highly qualified staff attorneys.
New Jersey	None	
New Mexico	Public Service Law Loan Repayment Assistance Program	The purpose of the New Mexico Public Service Law LRAP is to provide legal educational loan repayment assistance to individuals providing public service in state or local government or the nonprofit sector in New Mexico to low-income or underserved residents.
New York	New York State Bar Association Student Loan Assistance for the Public Interest	In recognition of the ever increasing need for attorneys in the field of public service, the New York State Bar Association created the Student Loan Assistance for the Public Interest (SLAPI) Program in 2002 to encourage new lawyers to pursue public service careers by providing financial assistance to attorneys who meet specified eligibility criteria, including qualifying employment and salary limitations.

ELIGIBILITY		
LICENSURE & EMPLOYMENT REQUIREMENTS	**INCOME**	**ELIGIBLE LOANS**
Applicants must be employed on a full-time basis with an approved nonprofit organization dedicated to serving the legal needs of low-income individuals and families in Montana, admitted to the State Bar of Montana by the end of the first year after having been selected as a participant.	The applicant's qualifying income may not exceed $40,000 to participate in the program. Qualifying income is defined as all income, including anticipated annual gross salary, minus $5,000 per dependent or amount of child support paid. If the applicant is married, the applicant will be treated as having the higher of (a) the applicant's individual income or (b) one-half of the combined income of both spouses.	The LRAP program covers only law school needs-based government or private loans, such as GSL, Law School Access (LAL), Law Loans and National Direct Student Loans (NDSL or Perkins Loans), as well as university or other private institutional loans associated with law school debt.
Attorneys employed by NHLA, LARC, DRC, or Pro Bono, full-time or part-time, who have outstanding law school loans are eligible. Assistance to part-time attorneys shall be prorated.	Not specified but income from other members of the household not taken into account	Only applies to law school debt, undergraduate debt not counted.
Requires three-year commitment to public service law. Applicant must have student law school loans that are not in default, applied to all available legal educational loan repayment programs offered by the applicant's law school for which the applicant qualifies, and be employed as a lawyer at an eligible employment site or be seeking employment at an eligible site.	Annual salary may not exceed $45,000.	Only applies to law school debt, undergraduate debt not counted.
Applicant must have graduated from an ABA accredited law school, been admitted to the New York State bar and be a member in good standing, and be employed full-time by a qualifying entity.	Income varies by years in qualifying employment and location.	Applies to debt incurred through institutional sources in pursuit of law school or joint legal and graduate school degrees.

continued on page 188

STATE	PROGRAM NAME	PROGRAM DESCRIPTION
North Carolina	North Carolina Legal Education Assistance Foundation Loan Repayment Assistance Program	To encourage and enable recent law school graduates to enter and remain in public service, the North Carolina LEAF sponsors an LRAP. The program's goal is to help remove the barriers to public interest practice faced by recent graduates who have incurred significant debt to finance their law school educations.
North Dakota	None	
Ohio	Ohio Legal Assistance Foundation Loan Repayment Assistance Program	Ohio Legal Assistance Foundation (OLAF) provides educational loan repayment assistance to attorneys employed by OLAF's grantee organizations in Ohio. The purpose of the program is to strengthen and expand civil legal assistance for the poor by supporting the recruitment and retention of qualifying attorneys by legal assistance programs funded by OLAF.
Oklahoma	None	
Oregon	Oregon State Bar Loan Repayment Assistance Program	The Oregon State Bar recognizes that substantial educational debt can create a financial barrier that prevents lawyers from pursuing or continuing careers in public service law. The Oregon State Bar's LRAP is intended to reduce that barrier for these economically disadvantaged lawyers, thereby making public service employment more feasible.
Pennsylvania	None	
Rhode Island	None	In 2003 a bill (H 5288) to create an LRAP was introduced to the Rhode Island General Assembly. As of November 2008 the bill had not passed.
South Carolina	Ness-Blatt Loan Repayment Assistance Program	The Foundation's LRAP name honors the public service commitment exemplified by Chief Justice Julius "Bubba" Ness and Speaker Sol Blatt.
South Dakota	None	

ELIGIBILITY		
LICENSURE & EMPLOYMENT REQUIREMENTS	**INCOME**	**ELIGIBLE LOANS**
Applicants must be a licensed member in good standing of the North Carolina state bar, have graduated in the last ten years from an ABA accredited law school, and work full time in a law-related public service job in North Carolina.	Income eligibility determined by years of practice. First-year attorneys may not make more than $42,000; second year attorneys $46,000; and attorneys who have practiced more than two years might not have an eligibility determination income of more than $51,000.	All need-based federal, university, and educational loans for law school education are eligible for inclusion in the program calculations so long as they meet the requirements of the loan repayment status.
Applicants must be licensed to practice law in Ohio within 18 months of participating in the LRAP and be employed by a nonprofit organization that provides free civil legal assistance to low-income individuals in Ohio and recieves funding directly or indirectly from OLAF. Participant may be employed full time or part time.	No financial eligibility requirements. OLAF will not reduce the amount of OLAF LRAP assistance due to receipt of other LRAP assistance.	Undergraduate, graduate, law school, and bar examination loans made by the government or an institutional provider for the education of the participant are eligible for repayment.
Applicants must be licensed to practice in Oregon and work within the state of Oregon for a qualifying employer. Part-time employees are eligible to apply for the program, but participation may be prorated at the discretion of the Advisory Committee.	Annual salary may not exceed $45,000.	All graduate and undergraduate educational debt in the applicant's name will be eligible for repayment assistance. Applicants with eligible debt at the time of initial application less than $30,000 willbe ineligible for program participation.
Lawyers who work for civil legal aid grantees of the Bar Foundation are eligible. Applications are distributed through the program directors or the grantees.	Not specified.	Not specified.

continued on page 190

STATE	PROGRAM NAME	PROGRAM DESCRIPTION
Tennessee	Program being developed	The Tennessee Legal Community Foundation has been awarded $103,597, which requires a dollar-for-dollar match, to create the Tennessee Loan Repayment Assistance Program for attorneys employed by nonprofit organizations providing civil legal services to low-income Tennesseans. The proceeds would be used to assist with the payment of loans incurred during law school.
Texas	Texas Student Loan Repayment Assistance Program	The Texas Access to Justice Commission (TATJC) created an LRAP to encourage and enable recent law school graduates to work for Texas legal aid organizations and to assist legal aid programs in retaining experienced lawyers.
Utah	None	
Vermont	Vermont Bar Foundation Loan Repayment Assistance Program	Vermont Bar Foundation's statewide LRAP provides loan assistance for licensed attorneys employed in nonprofit organizations dedicated to serving the civil legal needs of low-income individuals and families in Vermont or employed by the Offices of the Defender General or the State's Attorneys.
Virginia	None	
Washington	Washington State Bar Association Student Loan Repayment Assistance Program	Due to funding issues, the Washington State Bar Association's LRAP Advisory Committee is not opening the program to new applicants in 2008.
West Virginia	None	
Wisconsin	None	
Wyoming	None	

ELIGIBILITY		
LICENSURE & EMPLOYMENT REQUIREMENTS	**INCOME**	**ELIGIBLE LOANS**
Applicant must be licensed to practice law in Texas and be a member in good standing of the State Bar of Texas or be an immigration attorney (special restrictions apply). Applicant must be a full-time employee of an eligible organization and be a graduate of an ABA accredited law school within the last ten years. Those applicants eligible for loan repayment funds from other sources must apply to those programs for assistance as payors of first resort.	Applicant's household income will be considered in relation to the total of the applicant's student loan debt.	Applicant's undergraduate and law school debt, and debt incurred in joint degree programs, where one degree is a juris doctor, and all institutional loans used for educational expenses may be covered under this program.
Participants must be licensed to practice law in Vermont and be employed by a qualifying employer. Participants may be employed full time or part time. Assistance to part-time attorneys shall be prorated.	A participant's salary may not exceed $50,000.	Undergraduate, graduate, and law school loans will be considered in determining the amount of assistance.

State LRAPs: Loan Amounts and Contact Information*

STATE	ASSISTANCE		FUNDING OF PROGRAM
	AMOUNT	DURATION	
Alabama			
Alaska			
Arizona	Maximum of $10,000 annually, paid quarterly	Not specified	Not specified
Arkansas			
California			
Colorado			
Connecticut			
Delaware			
District of Columbia	Maximum of $12,000 per year with a $60,000 maximum	Unlimited duration but lifetime cap of $60,000	Funded by a grant from the DC City Council, IOLTA funds, and private contributions
Florida			
Georgia			
Hawaii			
Idaho			
Illinois			
Indiana	Maximum amount of $5,000 per year	Not specified	Foundation budgeted $50,000 for 2007-2008 LRAP-IN Program

*Current as of December 2008

LOANS	CONTACT INFORMATION	SOURCE OF INFORMATION
Loans are for one year and are forgivable at the end of the year.	Joannie.Collins@azflse.org	http://www.azflse.org/azflse/grants/loanrepayment.cfm
		http://www.abanet.org/legalservices/sclaid/lrap/statelraps.html
One-year loans, paid semiannually, are forgiven after 12-month service requirment.	DC Bar Foundation 2000 P Street, NW, Suite 530 Washington, DC 20036-6964 (202) 467-3750	http://www.dcbarfoundation.org/lrap.html
	Clara Bevington Florida Bar Foundation 250 South Orange Ave. Suite 600P Orlando, FL 32801 (407) 843-0045 (800) 541-2195 cbevington@flabarfndn.org	http://www.flabarfndn.org/content.php?page=33
		http://www.isba.org/publications/barnews/2008/11/assemblytoreview.html and http://www.abanet.org/legalservices/sclaid/lrap/statelraps.html
Annual loans are distributed quarterly and forgiven at the end of the annual award year.	Michael Tranovich Indiana Bar Foundation 230 E. Ohio Street Suite 400 Indianapolis, IN 46204 (317) 269-2415	http://www.inbf.org/Pages/documents/ProgramDescriptionandEligibility.pdf

continued on page 194

STATE	ASSISTANCE		FUNDING OF PROGRAM
	AMOUNT	**DURATION**	
Iowa	Maximum amount of $5,000 per year	Renewal applicants receive priority in consideration of future year awards. The number of years assistance will be provided to any participant will be determined in the future as the program grows and demand for assistance is evaluated.	The Iowa State Bar Association established this program with an initial investment of $25,000. The Iowa State Bar Association Foundation has generously matched that investment with an additional $25,000. Additional funding will be needed to continue the ISBA LRAP into the future.
Kansas			
Kentucky			
Louisiana	A maximum loan up to $5,000 per year, not to exceed 75% of the annual debt service on the eligible loans, may be awarded to each approved applicant.	Once accepted, an attorney may remain eligible for a maximum of five years.	The program is funded from the Louisiana Bar Foundation interest income reserves and private, supplemental sources.
Maine	Maximum of $5,000 for full-time attorneys. Prorated for part-time employment.	Maximum of ten-year participation.	Not specified
Maryland	Awards will be determined by an applicant's overall reported educational debt at the time of application. Recipients will lock in to an award level that contains set award amounts. Award funds are distributed annually over a three-year period as long as the recipient remains eligible and continues to submit the required annual employment, lender, and tax documentation by the September 30 deadline.	Three years	Not specified
Massachusetts			
Michigan			

LOANS	CONTACT INFORMATION	SOURCE OF INFORMATION
Loan assistance shall be paid quarterly and directly to the participant on a prospective basis.	Brett J. Toresdahl Executive Director ISBA Public Service Project (515) 244-8617	http://www.iowabar.org/miscdocuments. nsf/2b85a4ea12f4bfac8625669d006e27ab/ 24bff93d0fd0994b862574b0000beb22! OpenDocument
		http://www.abanet.org/legalservices/ sclaid/lrap/statelraps.html
Loans are made for one calendar year and are paid quarterly. Loans are forgivable at the end of the year.	Kevin Murphy Louisiana Bar Foundation 601 Saint Charles Ave 3rd Floor New Orleans, LA 70130 (504) 561-1046	http://www.raisingthebar.org/fundingprograms/lrap-guidelines.htm
Forgivable loans	M. Calien Lewis Executive Director Maine Bar Foundation (207) 622-3477	http://www.mbf.org/LRAP.htm
Award checks are issued with the applicant's name as well as the lender's name. Applicants are to endorse the check and forward it to the lender.	Tamika McKelvin Janet L. Hoffman Loan Assistance Repayment Program (LARP) Office of Student Financial Assistance Maryland Higher Education Commission State Scholarship Administration 839 Bestgate Road Suite 400 Annapolis, MD 21401-1781 (410) 260-4546	http://www.mhec.state.md.us/ financialAid/ProgramDescriptions/ prog_larp.asp
		http://www.abanet.org/legalservices/ sclaid/lrap/statelraps.html
		http://www.abanet.org/legalservices/ sclaid/lrap/statelraps.html

continued on page 196

STATE	ASSISTANCE		FUNDING OF PROGRAM
	AMOUNT	**DURATION**	
Minnesota	Loan amounts determined by Loan Committee.	Not specified	Not specified
Mississippi			
Missouri	Up to $4,000 per year	Recipients may apply for renewal benefits on a semi-annual basis for five years after entry into the program or until the year in which the educational loans are repaid in full, whichever occurs first.	Missouri Bar and the Missouri Bar Foundation
Montana	A maximum loan amount of $2,500 per year may be awarded to each approved applicant.	Maximum of five years	Private contributions and University of Montana School of Law
Nebraska			
Nevada			
New Hampshire	The program makes forgivable loans equivalent to a percentage of the total outstanding principal of all staff attorneys' law school loans. The formula and amount of assistance are subject to change annually, depending on the availability of funds and the aggregate extent of need shown on the annual applications.	Not specified	Not specified
New Jersey			

LOANS	CONTACT INFORMATION	SOURCE OF INFORMATION
Assistance is provided through forgivable loans. Loans will be forgiven following each calendar quarter, provided the recipient has remained in qualifying employment through the quarter and shows the required proof of repayment of qualifying student loans.	Heather Rastorfer Vlieger Executive Director Loan Repayment Assistance Program of MN, Inc. 600 Nicollet Mall, Ste. 380 Minneapolis, MN 55402 (612) 278-6315 HeatherRV@statebar. gen.mn.us	http://www.lrapmn.org/index.cfm?pagename=homepage
Awards are provided in the form of semiannual forgivable loans. Each loan is approved separately prior to issuance. Loans will be forgiven following each calendar half-year for which the loan was received, provided the recipient provides proof he or she has remained in qualifying employment through the half-year and shows proof that the LRAP loan was used to repay his or her qualifying student loans.	LRAP The Missouri Bar c/o Stephen Murrell PO Box 119 Jefferson City, MO 65102 (573) 635-4128	http://www.mobar.org/081bb76a-cdd6-44e7-a6bc-12c482b469e2.aspx
Loan disbursements will be made semiannually in April and November. Loan forgiveness will occur one year following the initial disbursement.	Amy Sing (406) 523-3920 asings@mtjustice.org	http://www.mtjustice.org/loan_repayment_assistance_program.htm
		http://www.ago.state.ne.us/news/pressreleases/081007_Nelnet_Agreement_II.htm
Loans under this program will be discharged by the Bar Foundation on certification that the recipients have provided services to NHLA, LARC, DRC, or Pro Bono. The Bar Foundation will then forgive the loans it has issued, forgiving one-quarter of each annual loan for each quarter of service provided during the applicable program year.	David G. Snyder (603) 715-3255 dsnyder@nhbarfoundation.org.	http://www.nhbarfoundation.org/Loan_Forgiveness.php

continued on page 198

STATE	ASSISTANCE		FUNDING OF PROGRAM
	AMOUNT	**DURATION**	
New Mexico	Up to $7,200 per year	Eligible for renewal	Not specified
New York	Up to $4,000 per year	Up to ten years	Grant from the New York Bar Foundation and donations from law firms
North Carolina	A participant must contribute a percentage of his or her eligibility determination income. NC LEAF will give the participant the remaining amount needed to meet his or her eligible debt repayment obligation, up to $9,000/year.	Duration not specified but participant must remain in qualifying employment for three years to receive forgiveness.	Sponsorships by law firms and other entities as well as other sources
North Dakota			
Ohio	$6,000 for full-time employees; part-time employees receive a prorated amount	An eligible attorney may receive a total of $75,000 from the OLAF LRAP during the lifetime of the program.	OLAF has made a commitment to funding LRAP at its current levels for multiple years, but continued operation and funding allocations are contingent on available funding and the number of eligible attorneys.
Oklahoma			
Oregon	LRAP loans will be $5,000 per year per program participant.	Maximum of three consecutive years	Not specified

LOANS	CONTACT INFORMATION	SOURCE OF INFORMATION
Not specified	New Mexico Higher Education Department Attn: Financial Aid Division 1068 Cerrillos Road Santa Fe, NM 87505	http://fin.hed.state.nm.us/content.asp?CustComKey=200291&CategoryKey=216320&WebFileKey=216324&pn=webfilesview&DomName=fin.hed.state.nm.us
Loan awards will be forgiven after three years of qualifying employment and subsequent schedule of forgiveness.	SLAPI, NYSBA One Elk Street, Albany, NY 12207 (518) 487-5641 probono@nysba.org	http://www.nysba.org/Content/NavigationMenu/ForAttorneys/ProBonoInformation/Student_Loan_Assista.htm
The program provides for no-interest loans in the first three years of public service employment, followed by loan forgiveness for continued public service.	NC LEAF NORTH CAROLINA LEGAL EDUCATION ASSISTANCE FOUNDATION Loan Repayment Assistance Program 3948 Browning Place Suite 334 Raleigh, NC 27609 (919) 845-6089 fax: (919) 848-9259 info@ncleaf.org	http://www.ncleaf.org/program.html
The LRAP assistance is provided in the form of a forgivable loan. Loans will be forgiven at the end of the year if the participant has been eligible all year.	Chuck Cook Director of Operations and Chief Financial Officer Ohio Legal Assistance Foundation 10 West Broad Street Suite 950 Columbus, OH 43215-3483 (614) 728-5396 ccook@olaf.org	http://www.lasnet.org/HR-Benefits/Information/LRAP_Guidelines_2008.pdf
The program will make a forgivable loan (LRAP loan) to program participants. The program annually will forgive one year of loans if the participant has been in qualifying employment the prior year and has paid at least the amount of his or her LRAP loan on his or her student loans. Only a complete year (12 months from, April 15, the due date of application) of qualifying employment counts toward LRAP loan forgiveness.	Catherine Petrecca (503) 431-6355 cpetrecca@osbar.org	http://www.osbar.org/lrap

continued on page 200

STATE	ASSISTANCE		FUNDING OF PROGRAM
	AMOUNT	**DURATION**	
Pennsylvania			
Rhode Island			
South Carolina	South Carolina Bar Foundation announced awards of $170,978 to 32 civil legal aid attorneys last year.	Not specified	Not specified
South Dakota			
Tennessee			
Texas	Applicants will be rank-ordered by TLC, from highest need to lowest need, based on the calculated student debt to income ratio.	SLRAP recipients may complete an abbreviated renewal application but will not receive automatic renewal or preference.	The Texas Student Loan Repayment Assistance Program (SLRAP) is administered by the Texas Access to Justice Foundation (TAJF) with funding from the State Bar of Texas, TAJF, and individual donors.
Utah			
Vermont	A maximum loan of $5,000 per year may be awarded to each approved participant. The number and amount of awards may be limited in the discretion of the Grants Committee of VBF-LRAP.	Former participants may apply in future award cycles if they have qualifying employment and income.	Not specified

LOANS	CONTACT INFORMATION	SOURCE OF INFORMATION
		http://www.abanet.org/legalservices/sclaid/lrap/statelraps.html
LRAP assistance is considered a forgivable loan. To have the loan forgiven, a participant shall complete a year of employment with a qualifying employer and make educational debt payments (interest and/or principal) that equal at least the amount of Foundation and other LRAP assistance received during the award year.	Jenny Brown South Carolina Bar Foundation PO Box 608 Columbia, SC 29202 (803) 765-0517 Fax: (803) 779-6126 jenny.brown@scbar.org	http://www.scbarfoundation.org/lrap.asp
		http://www.tsc.state.tn.us/GENINFO/PRESSREL/2007/074pr.htm
SLRAP loans are made to the recipients at no interest. Recipients must continue in their employment for one year following their first SLRAP disbursement to meet the objectives of the program and have their SLRAP loans forgiven.	Lawyers Care State Bar of Texas P.O. Box 12487 Austin, TX 78711 (800) 204-2222, extension 1855 (512) 427-1855 (in Austin) cnahay@texasbar.com	http://www.texasatj.org/programsservices/slrap/index.asp
Assistance will be disbursed in the form of a check equaling one-half of the total annual award amount. To receive the second check, the participant must submit proof of educational loan payments equaling half of the annual award amount during the first six months of the award cycle. Program assistance will, in no instance, be more than the amount of loan repayment paid by the participant.	Deborah Bailey Executive Director Vermont Bar Foundation P.O. Box 1170 Montpelier, VT 05601-1170 (802) 223-1400 dbailey@vtbarfndn.org	https://www.vtbar.org/

continued on page 202

STATE	ASSISTANCE		FUNDING OF PROGRAM
	AMOUNT	**DURATION**	
Virginia			
Washington			
West Virginia			
Wisconsin			
Wyoming			

LOANS	CONTACT INFORMATION	SOURCE OF INFORMATION
	WSBA Service Center 1325 Fourth Ave. Suite 600 Seattle, WA 98101-2539 (206) 443-9722 (800) 945-WSBA questions@wsba.org	http://www.wsba.org/lawyers/lrap.htm

Law School LRAPs

This appendix provides a list of law schools offering Loan Repayment Assistance Programs. The list and the average loan amounts were derived from the 2007-2008 E-Guide created by Equal Justice Works and available at their website, http://ejwguide. newsweek.com/guide/Results.aspx. Up-to-date and comprehensive information on law school LRAPs can be found at the websites of the respective law schools. For information on law school debt relief, an invaluable resource is Equal Justice Works at www.equaljusticeworks.org.

Law School	Average Annual Amount of Assistance
Albany Law School	Data unavailable
American University, Washington College of Law	$5143
Arizona State University College of Law	Data unavailable
University of Baltimore School of Law	Data unavailable
Boston University School of Law	$2980
University of California at Berkeley School of Law	$3679
University of California at Davis School of Law	$1177
University of California, Hastings College of Law	$2860
University of California at Los Angeles School of Law	Data unavailable
Capital University Law School	Data unavailable
Case Western Reserve University Law School	$5493
Charlotte School of Law	Data unavailable
University of Chicago Law School	Data unavailable
Chicago-Kent College of Law, Illinois Institute of Technology	$3500
Cleveland State University, Cleveland-Marshall College of Law	Data unavailable
University of Colorado School of Law	$1800
Columbia University School of Law	$8830
Cornell Law School	$6317

Law School	Average Annual Amount of Assistance
Creighton University School of Law	$1904
University of Denver College of Law	$8075
DePaul University College of Law	$5000
Duke University School of Law	$6052
Duquesne University School of Law	Data unavailable
Emory University School of Law	$2288
Fordham University School of Law	$2727
Franklin Pierce Law Center	$1560
George Washington University National Law Center	Data unavailable
Georgetown University Law Center	$5061
Golden Gate University School of Law	Data unavailable
Hamline University School of Law	Data unavailable
Harvard University Law School	$5689
Hofstra University School of Law	$2191
Indiana University School of Law — Bloomington	Data unavailable
University of Iowa College of Law	$3585
Lewis and Clark Law School	$4362
Loyola University School of Law, Chicago	$4000
Loyola Law School	$8333
Loyola University School of Law, New Orleans	Data unavailable
University of Maine School of Law	$7710
Marquette University Law School	$1878
University of Maryland School of Law	$7113
Mercer University Law School	$5000

continued on page 206

Law School	Average Annual Amount of Assistance
The University of Michigan Law School	$5343
University of Minnesota Law School	Data unavailable
University of Nebraska College of Law	Data unavailable
New York Law School	Data unavailable
University of North Carolina School of Law	Data unavailable
Northeastern University School of Law	$3639
Northwestern University School of Law	$3953
The Ohio State University College of Law	$3714
University of Oregon School of Law	Data unavailable
Pace University School of Law	$5000
University of Pennsylvania Law School	Data unavailable
The Pennsylvania State University, Dickinson School of Law	$4053
Pepperdine University School of Law	Data unavailable
Regent University School of Law	Data unavailable
Rutgers, The State University of New Jersey School of Law, Camden	$3212
Rutgers School of Law, Newark	$2796
St. Thomas University School of Law	Data unavailable
University of St. Thomas School of Law	$3514
University of San Diego School of Law	$7000
Seattle University School of Law	$2500
Seton Hall University School of Law	$1333
University of South Carolina School of Law	$2500
South Texas College of Law	Data unavailable

Law School	Average Annual Amount of Assistance
University of Southern California, Gould School of Law	Data unavailable
Stanford Law School	$10,000
Suffolk University Law School	$5565
Temple University School of Law	$2187
Touro College Jacob D. Fuchsberg Law Center	$3000
Tulane University School of Law	$6654
University of Utah, S.J. Quinney College of Law	$1425
Vanderbilt University School of Law	$2868
Vermont Law School	$3860
Villanova University School of Law	$2000
University of Virginia School of Law	$4395
Washington and Lee University School of Law	Data unavailable
Washington University School of Law	$2232
West Virginia University College of Law	Data unavailable
Whittier Law School	$1000
Widener University School of Law	$1612
Willamette University College of Law	Data unavailable
College of William and Mary, Marshall-Wythe School of Law	$3500
University of Wisconsin Law School	$2777
William Mitchell College of Law	$4210
Yale Law School	$7981
Yeshiva University, Benjamin N. Cardozo School of Law	$3703

Private LRAPs

Allegheny County Bar
Appalachian Research and Defense Fund of
   Kentucky's LRAP
Atlanta Legal Aid Society's LRAP
Center for Arkansas Legal Services' LRAP
Bay Area Legal Aid's LRAP
California Rural Legal Assistance's LRAP
Central Florida Legal Services' LRAP
Columbia Legal Services' LRAP
Community Legal Aid Services' LRAP (OH)
Community Legal Services' LRAP (AZ)
DNA-Peoples Legal Services LRAP
Florida Rural Legal Services' LRAP
Inland Counties Legal Services' LRAP
Lane County Legal Aid Services' LRAP
Legal Aid of Western Missouri's LRAP

Legal Aid Services of Oregon's LRAP
Legal Aid Society's LRAP (KY)
Legal Aid Society of San Diego's LRAP
Legal Services for Cape Cod & Islands' LRAP
Legal Services of Eastern Michigan's LRAP
Legal Services of North Florida's LRAP
Legal Services of Northern California's LRAP
Merrimack Valley Legal Services' LRAP
Montana Justice Foundation's LRAP
Neighborhood Legal Services of Los Angeles
   County's LRAP
Northwest Justice Project's LRAP
Ohio State Legal Services Association's LRAP
Southwest Virginia Legal Aid Society's LRAP
Texas Rural Legal Aid's LRAP
Virginia Legal Aid Society's LRAP
Volunteer Lawyers Project of the Boston Bar
   Association's LRAP

list from: http://www.lri.lsc.gov/sitepages/management/management_lrap.htm

Public Interest Law Resource Groups

ALLIANCE FOR JUSTICE (AFJ)

www.afj.org

AFJ Washington DC HQ
11 Dupont Circle NW
2nd Floor
Washington, DC 20036
Phone: 202-822-6070
Fax: 202-822-6068

AMERICAN CIVIL LIBERTIES UNION (ACLU)

www.aclu.org

ACLU-NCA Legal Committee
1400 20th St. NW, Suite 119
Washington, DC 20036
Phone: 202-457-0800

CENTER FOR LAW AND SOCIAL POLICY

www.clasp.org

1015 15th St. NW, Suite 400
Washington, DC 20005
Phone: 202-906-8000
Fax: 202-842-2885

EQUAL JUSTICE WORKS

www.EqualJusticeWorks.org

2120 L St. NW, Suite 450
Washington, DC 20037-1541
Phone: 202-466-3686

NEW YORK LAWYERS FOR THE PUBLIC INTEREST

www.nylpi.org

New York Lawyers for the Public Interest
151 West 30th St.
11th Floor
New York, NY 10001-4007
Phone: 212-244-4664
Fax: 212-244-4570
TDD: 212-244-3692

NAACP

www.naacpldf.org

NAACP Legal Defense and Educational Fund, Inc.
99 Hudson St., Suite 1600
New York, NY 10013
Phone: 212-965-2200

NATIONAL CENTER ON POVERTY LAW

www.povertylaw.org

National Center on Poverty Law
50 East Washington St.
Suite 500
Chicago, IL 60602
Phone: 312-263-3830

NATIONAL LAWYERS GUILD

www.nlg.org

National Lawyers Guild, National Office
132 Nassau St., # 922
New York, NY 10038
Phone: 212-679-5100
Fax: 212-679-2811

NATIONAL LEGAL AID AND DEFENDERS ASSOCIATION

www.nlada.org

National Legal Aid & Defenders Association
1140 Connecticut Ave. NW, Suite 900
Washington, DC 20036
Phone: 202-452-0620
Fax: 202-872-1031

PUBLIC INTEREST LAW INITIATIVE

www.pili-law.org

Public Interest Law Initiative (PILI)
c/o Foley and Lardner
321 North Clark St.
28th Floor
Chicago, IL 60654

Practical Tips

This appendix provides a list of practical tips for staying true to a commitment to public interest lawyering. I'm hesitant to detract from the inspiration and richness of the stories of the public interest lawyers contained in the preceding pages so I present the practical tips as a supplement and with a warning. There are no practical tips that can motivate you to stay true to your commitment if you are not determined. The analytical side of your brain can convince you to detour from your heart's desire if you allow the doubts to overwhelm you. The greatest practical tip I can give you is to trust the deep knowledge that you can succeed in being a public interest lawyer. The part of you that requires practical tips is not that deep knowing. Trust your heart. Follow the longing of your heart and soul. For the times the left side of your brain is the noisiest, though, here are some practical tips!

Prior to Law School

- Have a financial plan starting even before college that includes saving as much money as possible and borrowing as little money as possible.
- Have a contingency financial plan.
- Engage in gainful employment and save money.
- Avoid undergraduate educational debt to the extent feasible.
- Live simply.
- Research loan repayment assistance programs, at the law school level, state programs, and the federal loan forgiveness program. Have a plan.
- Get really good grades to increase your opportunity for law school scholarships.
- Research public interest programs at law schools you are interested in attending, including strong clinical programs.
- Investigate state schools to keep undergraduate debt low.
- Aggressively pursue scholarships and financial aid packages if attending a private law school.
- Take a year or two off between college and law school to work and save money for law school.

During Law School

- Develop relationships with advisors in the financial aid office of the law school.
- Pay close attention to how much money you're borrowing, knowing that every dollar adds up and will have to be paid back with interest.
- Maintain an accounting of how much debt you are accruing. Do not wait until spring semester of your third year to realize how much debt you're in.
- Avoid private debt wherever possible.
- Learn as much as you can about the federal loan forgiveness program, including when and how to consolidate your loans to guarantee eligibility for the program.
- Research loan consolidation plans to find the most favorable terms.
- Tap any and all public interest resources available.
- If the law school does not currently have a loan repayment assistance program, advocate for one.
- Seek out professors who teach public interest law or have a public interest law background and are passionate about justice issues.
- Find public-interest-minded role models.
- Create a support system around you of people who are planning to pursue public interest law or are already actively practicing public interest law. Find a community of supportive people with similar values.
- Do not let anything or anyone get in your way of pursuing your dream of being a public interest lawyer.
- Enroll in as many clinical legal education opportunities as possible.
- Become involved in a progressive, public-interest-oriented law journal.
- Work as much as possible during the school year and the summers to reduce the amount of loans you have to take out.
- Live with family or friends to minimize expenses and the amount of money borrowed.
- Stay true to your values and committed to your pursuit.
- Live simply.

After Law School

Finding a Job

- Think outside the box and outside the bigger, more expensive cities.
- Apply for fellowships that support lawyers working in the public interest.
- Find legal services and public interest law offices with loan repayment assistance plans and retirement plans.

- Research state loan repayment assistance plans in the states in which you are applying for jobs.
- Make sure you understand any loan deferral plans available.
- Find work you love to do.
- Understand the lifestyle choices you'll be making and accept having to live within your means.
- Know the procedure for qualifying for the federal loan forgiveness program and make certain you follow the procedure.

On the Job Working in Public Interest Law

- Create a realistic budget and stick to it.
- Use one of the financial management software systems available to track your spending and stay within your budget.
- Explore living with roommates to cut expenses.
- Resign yourself to living with your parents, if need be, for a year or two.
- Save money by bringing your lunch to work, taking public transportation, and shopping at thrift stores.
- Revel in the day-to-day successes and the satisfaction that comes from helping others.
- Remember that the clients you're representing are somehow getting by on far less income than you are receiving.
- Remember that money really cannot buy happiness. In fact, research has shown that, if you're motivated primarily by money, you're much more likely to be unhappy.
- Surround yourself with people involved in work they're passionate about.

On the Job Working in the Private Sector

- Research how pro-bono-friendly the law firm is and ask the hiring partner whether the firm supports associates' pro bono work.
- Become a member of the local bar association and the committee on pro bono of the bar association.
- Let the partners know that you're eager to take on pro bono cases.
- Seek out opportunities to become a board member of one or several not-for-profit corporations.
- Network through the local United Way or other established not-for-profit corporations to advance the firm's not-for-profit corporate practice.
- If you're working in the private sector temporarily to pay off loans, live on a public interest lawyer's salary and budget accordingly.

All the Time

- Follow your instincts.
- Trust yourself.
- Establish priorities.
- Don't let the money stop you.
- Don't be guided by fear and doubts.
- Keep your eye on the prize.
- Have no regrets.
- Know you can do it.
- Stay true to your ideals.
- Be authentic.
- Never compromise yourself or your values.